THE STORM WITHIN

MARK LITTLETON

Tyndale House Publishers, Inc.,
WHEATON, ILLINOIS

The "NIV" and "New International Version" trademarks are registered in the United States Patent and Trademark Office by International Bible Society. Use of either trademark requires the permission of International Bible Society.

Scripture quotations, unless otherwise noted, are from the Holy Bible, New International Version®. Copyright © 1973, 1978, 1984 International Bible Society. Used by permission of Zondervan Bible Publishers. All rights reserved.

Scripture quotations marked NASB are from the New American Standard Bible, copyright © 1960, 1962, 1963, 1968, 1971, 1972, 1973, 1975, 1977 by The Lockman Foundation. Used by permission.

Library of Congress Cataloging-in-Publication Data

Littleton, Mark, R., date
    The storm within / Mark R. Littleton.
        p. cm.
    Includes bibliographical references.
    ISBN 0-8423-7207-5 (SC) :
    1. Consolation. 2. Littleton, Mark R., date. 3. Depression, Mental—Patients—Biography. 4. Depression, Mental—Religious aspects—Christianity. I. Title.
BV4910.34.L58   1994
248.8'6—dc20   93-30564

Printed in the United States of America

99 98 97 96 95 94
8   7   6   5   4   3   2   1

To
Cliff Rapp
Bob and Susan Osburn and the minichurch
Larry and Donna Dyer
Bill and Debbie Peach
Kermit Horn
Nick Bartol
The class of '77 and the faculty of Dallas Seminary
Fellowship Bible Church and FBC Singles
The Minirth-Meier Clinic
—All friends without whose love and encouragement I might not be alive today

CONTENTS

INTRODUCTION

ANOTHER BOOK ON PAIN AND SUFFERING?

Why another book on suffering and pain?

There are many excellent books, tapes, and messages on the subject. Authors such as Joni Eareckson Tada, Philip Yancey, Edith Schaeffer, C. S. Lewis, and Billy Graham have written on the subject with eloquence, insight, clarity, and biblical accuracy.

What can I hope to add to the surfeit of literature already out there?

Frankly, I'm not sure, except to say that suffering and pain are problems that won't go away. No one has given the last word on the issue. Through another facet of insight perhaps I can help a few more "fellow plodders" make the journey of life without regret and bitterness, and even spur them on to the finish line in victory, as the apostle Paul wrote, with rejoicing.

We live in an age where nearly thirty thousand people in the United States commit suicide each year because of some form of unbearable pain in their lives. We are seeing the first tide of doctors who assist suffering people to die by their own hands so that their pain, they believe, will be ended. Pain and suffering are the glaring contradictions of living in a world with so much plenty, so much pleasure, so much reason to live. We ask why and get few satisfying answers. Now a few people are asking, "Why not just escape?" They find a way out through illegal drugs, legal medicines, and a multitude of diversions for every taste. Americans in particular find long-term, excruciating pain completely inexplicable. It is more often a reason not to believe in God than a potent impetus to turn to him for comfort and hope.

PAIN BEYOND THE NORM

My subject does have a slant. I write to speak to the issue of intense, overwhelming pain, a kind that is often accompanied by deep depression and a desire to die. Though pain of any variety can become intolerable, much of the kind of suffering we see in our world today is so intense and horrible we, even as observers at a distance, shrink from it. We just don't understand how a good, loving, and all-powerful God can allow certain kinds of pain to exist, let alone continue.

A friend of mine had a brother who recently died from complications from AIDS. He left her a fortune in life insurance, but she would rather have him back. She told me, "AIDS is a horrible, horrible death to die from. I was there when he died, and he kept his sense of humor. I asked him if he still loved me, and he laughed and said no. I knew he was joking, but what I witnessed I hope I never have to see again. His pain was so far beyond any I've ever seen anywhere. If I didn't believe in Jesus, I'd give up all hope."

Years ago, one of my dear uncles suffered from Parkinson's disease. In the hospital for a hernia operation, he was given the wrong medication. It lead to harrowing hallucinations and a terrible death. My mother told me afterwards, "Uncle Chuck died one of the worst deaths I've ever heard of. None of us understood the suffering God put that man and his family through. To this day I don't understand it. I believe God loves us, but that is one case I have to force myself not to think about."

More recently, as an elderly couple lost one of their closest friends to cancer, the wife said to me, "I'm losing all my friends, Mark. I never expected it would be like this. I may be the last one alive, and I don't know whether I can bear it."

I don't know about you, but I find "defending the faith" difficult under such conditions. We Christians feel we have to come up with some logical explanation of events and circumstances. But so many examples of pain defy explanation of any sort.

ANSWERS FOR THE DARK

Some answers have proven helpful. C. S. Lewis's oft-quoted aphorism is one. "Pain insists upon being attended to. God whispers to us in our pleasures, speaks in our conscience, and shouts in our pain. It is his megaphone to rouse a deaf world."

But what of a listening believer? He is not deaf, and yet he may be suffering intensely and intolerably. Studs Terkel writes in his book *American Dreams Lost and Found* of a onetime peace corps volunteer who worked in the Philippines. At the age of twenty-one the volunteer bore witness to women offering up their children to the Americans: "Take my child, take him with you to the States." The volunteer saw such actions by the thousands, and it was a tearing, heart-wrenching experience.[1] How does one reconcile himself to such suffering and the existence of a good, caring, all-powerful Christian God?

John Patrick, whose words I gleaned from a businessman's newsletter, said, "Pain makes man think. Thinking makes man wise. Wisdom makes life endurable."[2]

But wisdom can also be a source of great pain. The more knowledge one has, Solomon writes, the greater the sorrow. "For with much wisdom comes much sorrow; the more knowledge, the more grief" (Eccles. 1:18). Wisdom, gained through experience and observation, can drag the soul down like nothing else. The truly wise man sees reality most realistically and therefore, in some ways, horrifically.

This book, in that respect, is about going through a time of darkness so cold, stark, and unyielding that one may even feel forced to contemplate suicide as if it were the magic elixir to freedom. I write in particular to those going through the kind of darkness that compels them to question everything they have long believed about God, Christ, life, and eternity. Such times of darkness can envelope a person like smoke and choke off whatever belief in God he might have had. In one breath he asks,

"Why are you doing this to me?" and in the next, "Do you even exist?"

During my passage through that kind of darkness by means of a more than two-year clinical depression, those were the questions that raged in my soul. It was born out of a strong belief in God's sovereignty, goodness, love, and grace. If God was there, if God really ruled in the world and in my life as I believed, if God truly had a "plan" in which I had a specific role, and if nothing could ever happen to me—mentally, emotionally, physically—that God wasn't part of, then why was he allowing this to happen to me? My pain was characterized by a wrenching inability to serve him or even sense his presence. It left me high and dry upon a fiery beach of inner psychic pain. I could understand cancer or persecution or even paralysis. But depression made no sense. It took away everything that made life worth living, and it left in its place abominable feelings of self-destruction, inner hatred, doubt, and despair. It was entirely inexplicable. Where was God in the midst of this horror? Why had he "forsaken me"? And if he hadn't, why did it feel so very much as if he had?

Ultimately, I reasoned that if God wasn't involved, if God was not "there" in the sense that he was concerned enough to help me through it, then what good was he—in any part of life? If this part was closed off to him, what else was? If he couldn't fix this or work it for good, what good was the Bible, its promises, or any of its teachings? And if he wasn't there with me when I went "through the fire" as Isaiah said (43:2), if there was no sense of his protecting and loving presence, how could I be sure anything else in the Bible was true?

THE DARK NIGHT

Only years later, after that dark time, would I find out about something called "the dark night of the soul," spoken of primarily in Catholic mysticism and the writings of St. John of the Cross and Teresa of Avila. These two sixteenth-century mystics regarded the "dark night" as one of the highest points of Christian life, a momentous transformation that many of us will go through, an experience that has the power to raise us to altogether new levels of intimacy with God.

For years I have meditated on my own experience and what I have read by other authors concerning this dark night of the soul. Though I don't agree with St. John's rather narrow delineation of the experience, I've come to the conclusion that a "personal time of darkness" is not only an important and necessary element of true Christian growth, but also something that most (if not all) Christians will go through in some sense during their lives on earth.

WHAT IT IS

The dark night in my understanding does not necessarily mean clinical depression or an illness per se (as St. John of the Cross seemed to conceive of it). It is more likely any time of intense "spiritual testing" that leads to deeper questioning and searching, all of which results in emotional trauma. It can be a harrowing wilderness experience that pummels the believer through years of doubt and disillusionment. It can be a time of intense suffering—sudden paralysis, a painful bout with cancer, a time of vicious persecution, and perhaps even a painful personal failure of sin that seems to finish one for life in what he or she considered his or her calling.

WHERE WE'RE GOING

What is it that characterizes such a "night" of intense questioning, deep doubt, numbing despair, and terrifying personal isolation? I intend to show this in the pages ahead.

How does one cope in the midst of it? Again, keep reading. If we are to take such admonitions in Scripture as, "Blessed is the man who perseveres under trial" (James 1:12), "Do not be surprised at the fiery ordeal among you, which comes upon you for your testing, as though some strange thing were happening to you" (1 Pet. 4:12, NASB), and "We are considered as sheep to be slaughtered" (Rom. 8:36), then we can firmly conclude that every true Christian will be tested and "proven" as to the reality of his or her faith and love for God.

Above all, I want anyone who reads these pages to come away convinced that none of us is at the mercy of biochemistry, fate, circumstances, happenstance, chance, bacteria, enemies, or any other force we talk about every day. Rather, we are wholly in the hands of God. What we're going through is redemptive. It's not lost time, wasted life, a parenthesis on real living. No, a classic dark night of the soul is an experience designed to transform, elevate, and move us on and up the ladder of spiritual growth and commitment. It's something God in his wisdom and mercy uses for good, despite the maelstrom of evil that surrounds us.

Finally, I hope to encourage you to endure, to face the darkness and plod through it if necessary, without giving up. I find the words of Phillips Brooks, a famed American preacher living at the time of D. L. Moody and Charles Spurgeon, most inspiring: "The truest help which one can render to a man who has any of the inevitable burdens of life to carry is not to take his burden off, but to call out his best strength that he may be able to bear it."[3]

I cannot promise you a final answer to the question of pain. God has not given us one, and ultimately only he can answer it. But I can promise to give you some insight and help for the journey. It is a difficult road and not one without emotional and spiritual hazards. But it can be redeemed. God can use it for good. And ultimately, whatever losses or agonies we sustain in this world, we can be sure that this world is not the end. If it were, then pain and suffering would be the greatest enigma of all. But God has not left us without hope. I pray I can amplify that hope for you as you read these pages.

Endnotes
1. Studs Terkel, *American Dreams Lost and Found* (New York: Pantheon, 1980), 10.

2. John Patrick, *Bits and Pieces* (Fairfield, N.J.: The Economics Press), April 1979.

3. Phillips Brooks, *On Preaching* (Grand Rapids, Mich.: Baker, 1978), 179.

PART ONE

Emotional Obliteration!

Descent into Darkness

JOURNAL ENTRY— September 12

It has been three days now since this anxiety started. I keep
trying to pinpoint when it happened. The best I can say is it
seemed to begin while I was sitting in the student lounge
feeling envious of M—— laughing with his rather beautiful
fiancée over summer pictures. I distinctly remember telling
myself not to think or feel that way, and I forgot about it. But
it was as if some switch had been thrown in my psyche. Ever
since then I have felt desperately anxious and depressed,
though I can't seem to get a fix on what it is I'm anxious and
depressed about. Jane? Marriage? What?

It struck at a time when I should have been exceed-
ingly happy. I had signed up for courses with some of the best
profs at Dallas Seminary, where I was a third-year student. My
schedule was full, as I had always liked it. I was hitting the best
GPA I had ever had in my schooling. I had a new girlfriend. I had

come off the most effective, fruitful, and fulfilling summer of my
life as a ministry intern at the Evangelical Free Church of
Hershey, Pennsylvania, a church that had grown from a core
group of fifty people to more than a thousand in less than four
years.

Then I collided with a force inside me that I could not define
for weeks, which racked me with psychic pain so overwhelming I
began thinking of suicide almost from the start.

What I felt at first was an anxiety, then a surging torrent of psychic pain. I couldn't understand it. I knew Philippians 4:6-7: "Be
anxious for nothing," and 1 John 4:18: "There is no fear in love"
(NASB). I immediately applied those Scriptures to my problem.

But nothing changed.

I reached inside myself and did all the things I'd normally do
under such circumstances. I confessed any sin I could put a finger
on and thought that should be the end of it. I meditated on
appropriate Scriptures. I prayed and read my Bible. I absorbed
myself in my studies and my ministry.

But the dread feeling only stung deeper.

I went back over my actions and thoughts, and tried to find
the error.

But I couldn't spot any.

Why did I feel like this?

Deep down, I even told myself, "Emotions aren't important.
Don't worry about them."

But my emotions were gagging me. I could not "not worry
about them." They were taking over.

In just a few days I sank into a state of depression unlike anything I'd ever encountered. In another two days, I couldn't push
myself out of bed and I cut two classes—the first time in my
whole seminary career.

At the end of the week, I was considering self-destruction as
the only way out. Above all, I was asking, *Where is God?*

There was an acute sense of desolation, of desertion by heaven. His presence had disappeared, and I felt nothing of that warmth and peace that had been with me since my conversion.

What had happened? *How could he do this to me?* burned in my mind.

What the pain unleashed in my soul was revealed in the next few paragraphs of my journal that fall of 1975:

> It's an almost tangible feeling inside, like heat—like a heavy weight in my chest that feels empty, hollow, dark, and sweat-dripping hot. I can't figure this out. My arms get tight, and I have this swirling in the pit of my stomach. My mind feels afire with a constant gush of worries, doubts, recriminations—problems that haven't bothered me for years, especially since my conversion. It is like something inside me has broken, or as if some closet filled with monsters and horrid beasts has suddenly been thrown open. I feel constantly overwhelmed. Going to classes, hearing the assignments absolutely paralyzes me. Each one looks as difficult as climbing the Matterhorn bare-handed. Getting up in the morning is nearly impossible. My only escape is sleep. What is this? What is happening?
>
> I keep pleading with the Lord to restore me. I sense that something terrible has occurred and that I am unable to turn it around. What is more terrifying is that God may choose *not* to stop it. And what then?

What then? That was the pressing question I faced at that moment. If I couldn't stop it—whatever that unnameable inner feeling was—and God wouldn't, what then? The fear that I was "stuck" or that "this was 'it' for the rest of my life" roared inside my head like a maniacal banshee.

I would learn later that in psychiatric terms I was experiencing an "atypical clinical depression"—a form of depression that does not respond to anything but clinical and professional care. It was humiliating. I was mentally ill, an "emotional cripple," as one of my professors used to say.

I did not know it at the time, but I had just taken the first steps of a journey that would last more than two years, a journey that would involve the most intense suffering I have ever experienced.

HOW SWEET IT WAS

Coming to know Jesus Christ personally is the greatest thing that can happen to anyone. It was precisely that way for me. I found that he makes life meaningful, joyous, fulfilling. His presence is true security. Anyone who walks with him will know a blessedness of inner peace, calm, contentment, hope, and acceptance that makes the pleasures of our planet no contest. Through the ages countless leaders, authors, composers, artists, soldiers, and business people have testified to the difference Christ makes in a life.

Perhaps the fact that the "honeymoon" of life in Christ is such an exhilarating adventure is what makes suffering as a Christian so inexplicable. When you have had an intimate, life-transforming relationship with Jesus Christ that is suddenly turned on end and obliterated, you feel betrayed, annihilated in spirit.

My own first three years as a Christian after my conversion in August 1972 were days and months of wonder. Christ's coming into my life was a joyous, beautiful, overwhelming feeling of peace. For the first time in my life, I felt secure and forgiven. I knew now that I was loved, understood, and, above all, no longer alone. I was convinced there was nothing in life I couldn't face, because he and I would face it together.

That very first weekend, my life was revolutionized. In two days, I leaped from a lifelong commitment to evolutionism, hedonism, materialism, and agnosticism to an unswerving devotion to the Bible heaven and hell; Jesus; the wrongness of drugs, drunkenness, and promiscuity; and the rightness of good works, purity, and giving. I began to see in almost every circumstance of life the imprint of God's presence and love. "Coincidences" began happening on a daily basis that I immediately concluded were his handiwork. The fact that I needed a ride to the beach and a friend just "happened" to come by was one of his "little love gifts." A fellow traveler on the bus was a "divine appointment." That I "just ran into" old friends at the mall had been "planned from before the foundation of the world!"

Next I made another discovery: It only got better. The first fall and winter of my new life I got a job as a part-time chef and dishwasher at a ski resort on Stratton Mountain in Vermont. It was the fulfillment of a lifelong dream—to ski all winter—and it stunned me that God was in it. I thought he surely would prefer that I go to some remote island and convert the cannibals. But I found out God was "into" fun.

That winter I received a call to the ministry. I led several friends to Christ. Life had become an exciting joyride through enemy territory.

That first summer I worked in Wildwood, New Jersey, at a little evangelistic outreach center called Boardwalk Chapel. I found out about Calvinism, Arminianism, predestination, dispensationalism, and numerous other theologies too long to learn the definitions of. I fought theological battles, resigned myself to "truths" I didn't like, and tried to lead members of motorcycle gangs, beach people, drunks, and college coeds to Christ. That summer I was accepted at Dallas Theological Seminary against all odds and went there just a year after converting to Christ. I studied under men whose books I'd read and whom I'd heard on tape—men who would become exemplars for my life, true mentors and heroes.

My second year in seminary only enriched my understanding of this person who was at my side night and day. The next summer I interned as a youth pastor at the Evangelical Free Church of Hershey, which today is more than four thousand strong. The summer of '75, it was the record-setter on the block, and I had the greatest three months of my life. I went back to DTS convinced God had a special mission for me and my generation.

And then it struck.

DISASTER

What cracked into my psyche that September drained me mentally, emotionally, and spiritually. I wrote early on in my journal:

JOURNAL ENTRY— September 17
I have failed everyone. My parents. My family. Hershey Free Church. Fellowship Bible. DTS. The final truth is that I am an unequivocal failure, as a Christian and as a person. I wish God would just end it and get me out of here. I'm just a drain on society and useless. What's the point anymore?

Arrogant as it sounds, I began asking—with a vengeance—how such a thing could happen to such a decent Christian guy, and especially one who was destined to do so much for Christ in his world. After all, hadn't many people told me, "God's got a hold of you. You're going to do great things for him"? If they were even close to correct, why did God allow this thing to happen to me, let alone continue?

It was this question that has challenged and befuddled me for years. It ultimately led me to explore the meaning of suffering and even read St. John of the Cross and Teresa of Avila on the subject. I did not know it then, but I had entered a period that I now believe was the classical "dark night of the soul."

What Is a Dark Night of the Soul?

JOURNAL ENTRY— September 18

I think I know what hell is. Hell is utter and total separation from God forever, without hope, without change, without hope of change. The pain of that separation is so intense that one feels nothing but despair and anguish, "weeping and gnashing of teeth." I know I haven't truly been there. But I feel like it.

Dr. Rick Cornish, a pastor in Minnesota, who also went through what he considers "a dark night of the soul," struck a resounding chord with my own journal entry above. He said, "I don't want people to take this wrong. But when I was at the bottom of this experience, in abject and total misery and feeling like this was going to be my condition for the rest of my life, that despair so filled me that I felt I knew what hell was like. I believed in some sense I'd been there."

In the same way, such depression is more than a look

through the portals of hell; it is feeling as if you're there and can't get out.

So what is this thing called "the dark night of the soul?"

ST. JOHN OF THE CROSS

St. John of the Cross (1542–1591), a Spanish Carmelite monk, popularized the idea in the 1500s with his poem and commentary, which he never meant to be published, entitled *Dark Night of the Soul*. The small book is difficult reading. A thorough understanding of the history of Christian mysticism is almost a prerequisite. It is actually a guidebook designed to help young monks through an experience St. John believed was initiated, designed, and concluded by God to bring the seeker to a mountaintop-like union with the divine.

The book has two main sections preceded by a prologue poem St. John called "Stanzas of the Soul." It is a mystical rendition of the passage of the soul from "beginnerhood" in the monastic life to "the state of perfection, which is the union of love with God."[1]

St. John pressed on with two expositions of the poem. The first is the "dark night of the sense." This describes a time of "purgation" in which the beginner learns to shuck the bonds of the seven deadly sins through a probing, spiritually directive confrontation with his real nature. St. John intended to guide the beginner through a series of questions that would lay bare all his sins and lead him to triumph over them.

Once this purgation was under way, the joys of conversion and the mystical life-style would move toward a period of "aridity." Here, St. John offered the stronger "spiritual person" the insight that such an experience precedes the road to the "dark night." Of course, the seeker would desire the dark experience that would ultimately lead to a final illumination and union with God.

The second section, which St. John called the "dark night of the spirit," describes the heart of darkness itself. Some of the "torments" St. John listed are: "affliction," "pain in one's weakness," "the pains of hell," "profound emptiness," a "removal from all former happiness and a desire to go back to it," an "inability to receive support and instruction on spiritual matters," and the realization that "no one can help." Several passages sum it up this way: The seeker is "in such great pain and agony that the soul would find advantage and relief in death" (103).

"The soul feels itself to be perishing and melting away, in the presence and sight of its miseries, in a cruel spiritual death" (104).

The soul is brought into "anguish and, troubled in its heart, it suffers great pain and grief . . . it finds no consolation or support in any instruction nor in a spiritual matter" (110).

These intense moments of despair and anguish are punctuated occasionally by fleeting episodes of ecstasy. God allows this so that the soul "will not lose heart." Above all, St. John sees the event as a pit that eventually leads to a mountaintop: union with God and the experience of divine love.

Clearly, St. John is giving instruction to sturdy monastics, young men and women who lived in monasteries or convents and wholly devoted their lives to seeking God. He was a Carmelite, a mystical element of Spanish monasticism.

To sum up, St. John saw the dark night this way:

First, God personally brings about conditions that will purify the true seeker and open up the way to intimate knowledge of himself and his God.

Second, this knowledge and experience can only be gained through purging and suffering.

Third, the "dark night" is a period of spiritual trauma in which the believer's inner picture of himself and God is radically altered through a kind of spiritual surgery.

Fourth, the whole process from beginning to end is initiated and sustained by God himself. It cannot be produced by the seeker.

Remember that we are looking at an extremely mystical undercurrent within the river of Christianity. St. John of the Cross took his lead from previous writers such as Denys the Areopagite (fifth century), the English spiritual text *The Cloud of the Unknowing* (a "guidebook" to penetrating the heart of God through contemplative prayer), and the desert fathers (monks who withdrew into the desert to seek God in solitude).

St. Teresa of Avila

St. Teresa of Avila, another Spanish mystic and contemporary of St. John of the Cross, had a profound personal influence on him. She wrote of the idea of a dark night in her masterpiece, *Interior Castle*. In that book she laid out seven stages of spiritual growth that culminate in a dark night and then union with God. In one passage in the "Sixth Mansions" chapter, she said,

> In due course [the soul] gets troubled again. . . . The thing grows almost intolerable, especially when on top of everything else come periods of aridity, during which the soul feels as if it has never known God and never will know Him. There are many things which assault her soul with an interior oppression so keenly felt and so intolerable that I do not know to what it can be compared, save to the torment of those who suffer hell, for in this spiritual tempest no consolation is possible.[2]

All this is very foreign to our modern concept of spiritual life. Many of today's Christians concentrate on "the abundant life," victory, productivity, and "making things happen," rather than with seeking an intimacy with God that may call for intense suffering and pain. In fact, I am convinced many of us are so sure that God wants us to live happy, healthy, wholistic, and joyous lives that when troubles assault us, we immediately challenge him, saying, "Why did you let this happen?" and "What did I do to deserve this?"

This overlooks the truth that God is far more concerned about developing us in holiness than in happiness. Some read books on suffering and are inspired, but we tend to think that is only for the chosen few. We certainly do not want to experience such things ourselves.

THE BIBLE ON THE DARK NIGHT

Nonetheless, there is clear precedent for such experiences in Scripture. In many instances, the saints of God attained personal growth and understanding through suffering such as St. John of the Cross pictures. Consider this list of some of biblical people who went through a time of tremendous spiritual darkness that probably involved melancholy, depression, and despair:

Job—naturally, the greatest example of suffering and darkness
Abraham—waiting for a son to be born through Sarah (His struggles are documented in Genesis simply as episodes, but behind it all one can see the personal darkness and lack of understanding he felt.)
Jacob—his battle with Esau, and the wrestling with the angel
Joseph—during his rejection, slavery, and imprisonment
Moses—forty years in the wilderness alone, before the Exodus
Israel (as a nation)—during the years in the wilderness
Samson—in his blindness and final suicide
David—while fleeing from Saul, and after his adultery with Bathsheba; many Psalms portray the anguish he suffered
Solomon—much of Ecclesiastes shows his personal battle for faith and a sense of meaning in life
Elijah—his desiring suicide after the duel on Mount Carmel with the prophets of Baal when Jezebel threatened his life
Jeremiah—during various imprisonments and rejections

Jonah—his sojourn in the belly of the fish and thereafter is a picture of the prophet facing his own disappointment with God

Daniel—his anguish and pain is revealed many times in his book

Hosea—through Gomer's adulteries and Hosea's confusion over what God was doing

Jesus—in the wilderness with the devil, in Gethsemane, and on the cross

Paul—2 Corinthians 1 reveals his own memory of personal anguish; also 2 Corinthians 12 and other passages

In all these cases, the suffering can be defined particularly as an experience of inner anguish, despair, spiritual torment, and a sense of separation from God, accompanied by deep theological questioning. Some people above suffered because of sin (David, Jonah, Samson). But most of them seemed to suffer as part and parcel of being human. What of those who didn't sin? Was their pain brought about or allowed for some spiritual purpose?

REASONS FOR SUFFERING

Scripture reveals a number of specific reasons why both believers and unbelievers suffer. For instance, suffering can be God's means to motivate an unbeliever to change and stop living sinfully (Eph. 5:6), as well as a means to bring him or her to salvation (Jonah 1:13, 16).

Sinful Christians suffer at times to discipline them and bring them back to spiritual living (Heb. 12:6). Suffering can also be the consequence of previous sin, even of those sins of which they've repented. The best example of this is King David who was "repaid" four times for his transgression with Bathsheba and the murder of Uriah. There is also John's difficult reference to a final penalty of death for those Christians who continue in sin (1 John 5:16). In all these cases, repentance is God's desired goal.

But what of non-sinning and innocent believers? Here the list is far more extensive. Consider these reasons Scripture offers for suffering and pain.

We suffer:

- so God may teach us patience (James 1:3).
- so God may motivate us to obey (Heb. 5:8).
- so that we might comfort and encourage others (2 Cor. 1:6).
- to keep us from sin (2 Cor. 12:7).
- so that we may glorify God (1 Pet. 4:16).
- so that we may share Christ's suffering (Phil. 3:10).
- so our faith may be strengthened (1 Pet. 5:10).
- so that others will be saved (2 Tim. 2:10).
- to conform us to Christ's image (Rom. 8:28-29).
- to teach others how to comfort us (2 Cor. 2:1-7).
- to move others to pray (2 Cor. 1:10-11).
- to motivate us to learn to go to God for help (Ps. 30:6-7).
- to allow us a special experience of God's presence (James 4:6-7).

Undoubtedly, there are other reasons. One not listed above, though, is a particularly difficult one, and it is found in the story of Job. It is this: We may never know why we suffer! Job didn't, even though we, as readers of his story, do.

Nonetheless, these reasons, while instructive, seem a bit dry and clinical. They do give us a sense of why we suffer—so that God may attain some or many of the above ends. But ultimately, we can come back to the old standard, that suffering is a means to spiritual growth.

Again, this is somewhat vague. Speaking practically, *everything* in life is (or can be) a means to spiritual growth. Certainly the truth that God "works all things together for good" applies to all circumstances for the believer.

Knowing this does not make suffering any easier. And it does not explain the experience of intense, overwhelming suffering

that we find so often in the modern world. It also doesn't answer
the question we ask when we suffer: "Is this from God to make
me grow?" When we are caught in the middle of deep and even
excruciating pain, knowing that this is God's means of making me
grow is almost laughable! "I became a quadriplegic so I can grow
as a person?" "I went through a depression that almost ended in
suicide to help me *grow?*" "My father died prematurely so he and
we could GROW?"

In a word, isn't there a better way?

In fact, there may not be! The army still believes the rigors of
boot camp are the best way to introduce young men and women
to the military. In college, while some methods change, there are
not many ways to educate students except through hard, concen-
trated study. (We still haven't found a way to "infuse" knowledge
using a tape recorder under the pillow!) Pain is still the best warning signal of medical problems. And suffering may be the only
way for God to teach us real love and obedience.

Somehow, though, the answers aren't very satisfying, partly
because it is so hard to see growth when we are on our back in
mortal pain, and partly because it is such a grinding platitude. We
want something loftier, something with true grit, something that
engages the spirit and inspires!

Maybe in the end, though, such an answer isn't possible. Jesus
learned obedience through the things that he suffered, and ultimately that kind of obedience is precious, powerful, and a worthy
gift. After all, is such obedience and character easy to produce?
Anyone who has raised children knows it is not. Real character—
the kind that God wants to build into us—requires the utmost in
spiritual training and discipline. It doesn't happen with a single
command or a snapping of the fingers. Every sports coach knows
what it takes to transform a kid off the street into a team player.
Every seasoned lawyer knows that a courtroom master doesn't
appear by chance. Ultimately, if it takes suffering of the kind that

Jesus and all these others went through to reach God's goals, then why not? Why shouldn't God use it as the most formidable of all his tools in making us like Christ?

This becomes an especially powerful truth when we compare it to the alternative. What is suffering for the unbeliever? It is nothing more than rank evil, pain that should be avoided and escaped. But what if you can't avoid it and escape? Then it is sheer tragedy. It has no redemptive value. It is a waste.

You can also compare the "Christian" explanation to that of other religions, and you find a similar difficulty. In Hinduism, pain is a punishment for sins of a previous life. In Buddhism, only self-induced pain has value; pain that comes upon us from outside is again punishment. Christian Science looks at pain as an illusion that must be overcome. Only in Christianity is pain a positive, something that is redemptive and can be used for good.

That brings us again to the dark night. As one of God's most potent tools, does it work?

RHYTHM

Howard Baker, president of Spirituality Resources, a mentoring and counseling ministry in Denver, Colorado, directed my thinking in this matter. In moving a Christian through a lifetime of growth intended to enable him or her to "glorify God and enjoy him forever," God often works through two primary processes: consolation and desolation. "Consolation" is God's comfort through his spiritual presence so that the believer senses a deep inner security; he knows he is not alone and never will be.

In "desolation" God tests and proves saints. It is the opposite of consolation, for in desolation God seems absent, as if he has purposely withdrawn from us. We feel a distance.

Reverend Baker commented, "It is a foreign concept in modern evangelicalism. A common 'maxim' we use is the question, 'If you don't feel close to God, who moved?' But the mystic's con-

cept of the absence of God, a conscious and divinely caused abandonment, is a way that I believe God works to transform us. It's
what I call the 'rhythm of spiritual life.'"

Such a dark night, whether it appears as illness, persecution, failure, the death of long-held dreams, or even a kind of mid-life crisis, is in some sense allowed by God. Without resorting to evil
intent, or even causing evil to happen, God uses the dark night
experience to build the believer in ways that could not happen
without it.

It is an utterly theological experience. God has emotionally
and mentally disappeared from the sufferer's universe, so the sufferer is forced to ask, "How do I know objectively that God even
exists?" The sufferer is forced to reckon with the towering question, "How do I know Christianity is really the truth?" Christ is
distant, unreal, and seemingly uncaring. The sufferer often cries,
"How do I know Jesus was who he said he was? How do I know
he really rose from the dead? How do I know this dying for sins
is the truth?"

All these questions envelop his mind in a dark cloud of doubt,
fear, and anxiety. Thus it is when everything is stripped away,
when his emotions have rendered every certainty uncertain, then
he discovers his true commitments. If he is truly God's child, he
will persevere; he will find real, objective answers to his difficulties. He will endure the pain and despair and seek to obey, even
though he cannot feel an iota of joy in his obedience. He will
emerge stronger in faith, better able to handle life's traumas with
compassion for others and personal reliance on God. He will, in
many ways, fear nothing in this world save God himself.

And if he does not work through these questions? More than
likely he will depart from the faith (as Saul did) or simply give up
and realize Christianity wasn't for him anyway. In extreme cases,
he might go insane (as Nietzsche did) or commit suicide (as King
Saul, Ahithophel, and Judas Iscariot did).

That is not a happy picture. There are casualties. The pain for some leads to terrible consequences.

Obviously, much would be at stake if God's "plan for the ages," could not be accomplished. If he is not able to keep his promises of preserving us until the end, we would have a right to question whether he is worthy of our love, trust, and worship. His holiness and integrity would be brutally compromised. Surely God somewhere has the answer.

Endnotes

1. St. John of the Cross, *Dark Night of the Soul,* trans. and ed. E. Allison Peers (Garden City, N.Y.: Image Books, 1959), 35.

2. St. Teresa of Avila, *Interior Castle,* trans. and ed. E. Allison Peers (Garden City, N.Y.: Image Books, 1961), 131.

THREE

The Dark Night of the Soul in Today's World

JOURNAL ENTRY— September 16

At times I think I am cracking up; my personality has disintegrated, and I will soon be placed in a mental institution. My body is continually racked with the pain of deep tension and fear. The physical sensation of something sharp and gouging passing through my inner organs is so real I have at times looked at my belly just to check. I doubt repeatedly that God even exists. I feel no longer certain of anything. I keep saying, "I believe" inside just to make sure he doesn't think I don't and get really mad.

Foremost among those in the Christian tradition who have undergone some kind of dark night is Martin Luther (1483–1546). One of the famous stories connected with his own perennial battle with depression and despair comes from an anecdote about how Luther's wife, Katherine, appeared in his study dressed in black as if she was in mourning. Luther gazed at her, astonished. "Woman, who is dead?"

"God is dead," she soberly replied.

Laying down his pen, Luther answered, "My soul, why do you speak of God being dead?"

"You have been acting that way," she said, "as though all hope were gone and God was dead."

Luther is said to have snapped out of it through his wife's comic intervention. Prior to Luther's conversion, he often beat himself senseless with a whip in his monk's cell. He felt horror and guilt over his sin. He quaked with anxiety in taking the Eucharist, and when he was finally ordained to serve it, he was terrified and shook like a man in a gale. At that time, Luther had not yet come to true faith in Christ.

In that respect, such a dark night can actually lead to conversion.

David Brainerd (1718–1747) kept a well-known journal of his own experiences as a missionary to the Indians of eastern Pennsylvania. The years 1743 and 1744 were particularly difficult. Some entries from that journal read:

> April 7: Appeared to myself exceedingly ignorant, weak, helpless, unworthy, and altogether unequal to my work. It seemed to me that I should never do any service, or have any success among the Indians. My soul was weary of my life. I longed for death, beyond measure. . . .

> April 16: I retired and poured out my soul to God for mercy, but without any sensible relief. . . .

> April 20: Set apart this day for fasting and prayer, to bow my soul before God for the bestowment of divine grace; especially that all my spiritual afflictions, and inward distresses, might be sanctified to my soul. . . .

May 10: Was in the same state as to my mind, that I have been in for some time; extremely oppressed with a sense of guilt, pollution, and blindness. . . .

July 25: Had little or no resolution for a life of holiness, was ready almost to renounce any hope of living to God. And O how dark it looked, to think of being unholy forever![1]

While Brainerd obviously suffered from depression as part of his personality, his diary reveals a man in daily crisis. He fought constant inner battles with a fearsome darkness that were punctuated by moments of sublime ecstasy.

Again, could God have been allowing him to go through times of desolation to hone him for the wide ministry he would have for centuries after through his diary?

Charles Spurgeon (1834–1892) was one of history's greatest preachers. Yet, he frequently told his listeners, "I am the subject of depressions of spirit so fearful that I hope none of you ever get to such extremes of wretchedness as I go to."[2]

On a number of occasions he sought refuge from his own darkness by taking lengthy vacations in Mentone, France, the warmest town on the Riviera.

These people are all potent examples of one fact. God not only does not spare his own from suffering, but certain of them he seems to put through greater suffering than others, just to train them in the kind of obedience and commitment so necessary for a wide ministry.

MORE RECENTLY

In recent years, others have written of this dark night experience, even though they have not defined it that way. C. S. Lewis, for instance, is one who was intimately familiar with the time of "desolation." This passage from his famous fictional correspondence between two demons, *The Screwtape Letters,* illustrates his own perception of it:

> It may surprise you that in His efforts to get permanent pos-
> session of a soul, He relies on the troughs even more than
> on the peaks; some of His special favorites have gone
> through longer and deeper troughs than anyone else. The
> reason is this. To us a human is primarily food; our aim is
> the absorption of its will into ours, the increase of our own
> area of selfhood at its expense. But the obedience which the
> Enemy demands of men is quite a different thing. One must
> face the fact that all the talk about His love for men, and
> His service being perfect freedom, is not (as one would
> gladly believe) mere propaganda, but an appalling truth. He
> really does want to fill the universe with a lot of loathsome
> little replicas of Himself—creatures whose life, on its minia-
> ture scale, will be qualitatively like His own, not because He
> has absorbed them but because their wills freely conform to
> His. We want cattle who can finally become food; He wants
> servants who can finally become sons. . . .
>
> And that is where the troughs come in. He is prepared to
> do a little overriding at the beginning. He will set them off
> with communications of His presence which, though faint,
> seem great to them, with emotional sweetness, and easy con-
> quest over temptation. But He never allows this state of
> affairs to last long. Sooner or later He withdraws, if not in
> fact, at least from their conscious experience, all those sup-
> ports and incentives. He leaves the creature to stand up on
> its own legs—to carry out from the will alone duties that
> have lost all relish. It is during such trough periods, much
> more than during the peak periods, that it is growing into
> the sort of creature He wants it to be. Hence the prayers

offered in the state of dryness are those which please Him best.[3]

What are these "troughs" if not the rhythm of consolation and desolation that Howard Baker suggested? Couldn't a deep trough be the true "dark night"?

Now look at this text from Lewis's *A Grief Observed*, the author's own experience with a devastating "trough" after the death of his wife:

> Bridge-players tell me that there must be some money on the game, "or else people won't take it seriously." Apparently it's like that. Your bid—for God or no God, for a good God or the Cosmic Sadist, for eternal life or nonentity—will not be serious if nothing much is staked on it. And you will never discover how serious it was until the stakes are raised horribly high; until you find that you are playing not for counters or for sixpences but for every penny you have in the world. Nothing less will shake a man—or at any rate a man like me—out of his merely verbal thinking and his merely notional beliefs. He has to be knocked silly before he comes to his senses. Only torture will bring out the truth. Only under torture does he discover himself.[4]

What can these "horribly high" stakes be but a time in which your own will to live and everything you believe is sorely and intensely tested to the limit? I now believe Lewis was experiencing a true dark night as his own faith was shattered and rebuilt through his recovery from the loss of his wife.

A MISTAKE TO AVOID

Dr. Eugene Peterson, another devotional writer on the spiritual life, says this in one of his books:

The only serious mistake we can make when illness comes, when anxiety threatens, when conflict disturbs our relationships with others is to conclude that God has gotten bored in looking after us and has shifted his attention to a more exciting Christian, or that God has become disgusted with our meandering obedience and decided to let us fend for ourselves for awhile, or that God has gotten too busy fulfilling prophecy in the Middle East to take time now to sort out the complicated mess we have gotten ourselves into. That is the only serious mistake we can make. It is the mistake that Psalm 121 prevents: the mistake of supposing that God's interest in us waxes and wanes in response to our spiritual temperature.[5]

Peterson recognizes the ebb and flow of spiritual life, and especially in a time of serious trial. As emotional creatures, we might suppose that just as we are "in God's image," so "God is in our image." Not so. We correspond to certain elements of his nature, but we are not a complete portrait. Just as God's thoughts are not our thoughts, so his emotions are not ours. While we may feel separated from him, it is just that: a feeling. A persistent perception of desolation does not mean he has deserted us. But it can feel that way, and intensely so.

Pastor Don Baker describes his own experience with deep depression in his book *Depression:*

For hours each day I would ponder such questions as: "Where is God?" "Why doesn't He answer me?" "Has God really deserted me?"

My theology rejected the last possibility, but my life seemingly had nothing to show for His abiding presence.

My Bible kept saying to me that God is a changeless God, and yet it seemed that without explanation He suddenly had become terribly indifferent.

This God of mine, who had promised never to leave or forsake me, appeared now to be playing some cruel form of hide and seek. No matter how diligently I sought Him, He was nowhere to be found.

This God whom I had loved and served had promised to keep His ears ever open to my cries. When I prayed, however, it seemed that He had now become stone deaf.

My Bible, always a source of strength, had little to say to me. When it did speak, the words were soon lost in the pall of gloom and forgetfulness that had settled down over my mind.

Time and again I would leaf through its pages, seeking a promise or an explanation, only to close its covers in disappointment.

Martha brought me a book by Andrew Murray, one of my favorite authors, entitled *Abiding in Christ*. The cover picture was that of an earnest Christian kneeling beside a chair, apparently agonizing in prayer.

I studied the picture for a few moments and then threw the book across the room in disgust.[6]

ONE ON HIS FEET DANCIN'

Another man that I believe has traveled through the dark night is Tim Hansel, whose popular book *You Gotta Keep Dancin'* reveals much of his thinking as he trekked through his own pain:

I realize that for days I have been so self-preoccupied that I have closed out all the windows of light. Help me to will your will, Lord. Help me to get outside of my own puny preoccupations (33).

I feel like I'm in a walking coma. Coherence eludes me. Sometimes it's almost frightening to close my eyes and sleep, for fear that I might not wake up. Oftentimes during the day, I have real difficulty staying conscious. I know neither what is wrong with me nor what is keeping me going. However, if these symptoms continue, I will probably ask to be hospitalized again. I'm sure that the strain on Pam is becoming almost unbearable. I have tried with all my limited endurance to show no signs of my discomfort for the past many months, but I think my disguise has worn thin (34).

Tonight—another night of not being able to sleep for the pain and symptoms—it's all moving to proportions that I can no longer handle.[7]

PHYSICIAN AND/OR EMOTIONAL PARALYSIS

Another obvious choice is Joni Eareckson Tada. In her book *Joni,* she reveals the story of that pain-racked three years recovering from the accident that left her a quadriplegic for life. Philip Yancey interviewed her while writing his book on pain, *Where Is God When It Hurts?* He writes:

> Joni found her condition impossible to reconcile with her faith in a loving God. It seemed all God's gifts, the good things she had enjoyed as an active teenager, had been stolen from her. What did she have left?
>
> The turning to God was slow. Change from bitterness to trust in Him dragged out over three years of tears and violent questionings.[8]

POINTS OF CONTINUITY

While none of these writers relate their sufferings to St. John of the Cross's dark night of the soul, there are these qualities in them all:

- A sense of God's distance and yet a determination to pursue and find him in the midst of it
- A compelling theological battle over God's goodness, love, grace, presence, care, compassion, and sovereignty
- Overwhelming feelings of inner distress, despair, and a deep sense of divine abandonment

All these are elements of St. John's "dark night" as well as the way I have tried to define it. Many committed Christian men and women have written on spiritual life and how God orchestrates true Christlikeness in his people. The Scriptures show us a multitude of tools the Spirit of God can use to transform each of us. Spiritual disciplines (prayer, fasting, study, meditation, prostration, solitude, serenity, silence), circumstances (sickness, failure, persecution, trials), and personal struggles (doubt, depression, despair, temptation, loneliness, anxiety, worry, fear) all contribute to shape us and mold us in God's hands.

However, as all these people testify, there clearly are times when God allows his children to go through a darkness so overwhelming that they can do little more than weep and cry out for relief. Such a situation is what I call the dark night of the soul. It is, I believe, a tool the Spirit of God uses to perfect his saints and bring about that capacity to "glorify God and enjoy him forever."

ITS IMPORTANCE

Why is this so important? Because, had someone told me that during my own agonizing experience with depression I could be experiencing the classic dark night of the soul, I might have endured with greater determination than I did. Perhaps my attitude would have reached for what St. John of the Cross sought: an inner sense of willing endurance. Above all, I would have understood that this was something God allowed for a purpose, which he would use to transform me, and which would produce spiritual fruit in my life that would truly redeem it.

Had I known I might be undergoing what Job, Moses, David, Solomon, Jeremiah, Habakkuk, Jesus, and Paul experienced to refine and strengthen them as the children of God, it might have been that much more tolerable and survivable (though probably not any the less painful).

But no one told me.

No one even hinted at it.

I wish they had. It might have made the questions in my mind a bearable howl rather than the ghoulish scream they became.

Perhaps.

I can't really be sure. Living through such darkness is not only inner anguish, but anguish produced by the conviction that it will never end. If I did not have that sense of "this will never change—you will never get better," perhaps the dark night would have ceased to be a dark night.

Still, knowing about the dark night produces an understanding that enables us to believe it is a redemptive experience. As a friend of mine says, "God never wastes suffering." God will use it for good in our lives. It will end. And when we emerge at its end, we will know a glory and an intimacy with God that surpasses all that has gone before.

William Styron echoes a similar, though much darker sentiment in his eloquent analysis of his own depression, *Darkness Visible: A Memoir of Madness:*

> If depression had no termination, then suicide would, indeed, be the only remedy. But one need not sound the false or inspirational note to stress the truth that depression is not the soul's annihilation; men and women who have recovered from the disease—and they are countless—bear

witness to what is probably its only saving grace: it is con-querable[9]

The dark night is survivable and redeemable. God does not waste your or my suffering. He uses it for good. He hones and guides it so that it produces a God-desired result. He is there while we're going through it, and he never lets go. But part of the process is the necessary feeling that he is not there. It is only through that experience that we arrive at our real convictions about God, life, love, liberty, and what is of value in this world. It is then that we truly approach the kind of maturity and commit-ment he longs to see in us.

There is the story of Auguste Renoir, the famed French Impressionist painter, who in his last years suffered from arthritis and paralysis in his limbs. The painter, though, did not complain; he continued to paint despite the agony. One day, the younger Henri Matisse, also an Impressionist and one who goes down in history as an equal of Renoir's, asked the famed artist, "Auguste, why do you continue to paint when you are in such agony?" Renoir answered, "The pain passes, but the beauty remains." He continued this to his last days, and one of his greatest paintings, "The Bathers," was completed two years before his death, four-teen years after contracting his terrible illness.

"The pain passes, but the beauty remains." James echoes the same thought: "Blessed is the man who perseveres under trial, because when he has stood the test, he will receive the crown of life that God has promised to those who love him" (James 1:12).

There truly is a crown of life at the end of the dark night. A crown that is "life" itself. A crown that gives life and makes life that much more bounteous and beautiful.

But it only comes through such a trial. Not before it or with-out it.

Endnotes

1. David Brainerd, *Life and Diary of David Brainerd* (Newark, Del.: Cornerstone Publishing Co., n.d.), 21–23.

2. Warren W. Wiersbe, *Giant Steps,* ed. Warren W. Wiersbe (Grand Rapids, Mich.: Baker, 1981), 263.

3. C. S. Lewis, *The Screwtape Letters* (Washington, D.C.: Christianity Today, Inc., 1969), 37–38.

4. C. S. Lewis, *A Grief Observed* (New York: Bantam Books, 1976), 43.

5. Eugene H. Peterson, *A Long Obedience in the Same Direction* (Downers Grove, Ill.: InterVarsity Press, 1980), 39.

6. Don Baker and Emery Nester, *Depression* (Portland, Oreg.: Multnomah Press, 1983), 65–66.

7. Tim Hansel, *You Gotta Keep Dancin'* (Elgin, Ill.: David C. Cook, 1985), 33–34.

8. Philip Yancey, *Where Is God When It Hurts?* (Grand Rapids, Mich.: Zondervan, 1977), 118.

9. William Styron, *Darkness Visible: A Memoir of Madness* (New York: Random House, 1990), 84.

FOUR

Depression and the Dark Night of the Soul

JOURNAL ENTRY— September 18

I have learned to call what's happening depression. The turmoil I feel inside is virtually unending. How can it go on like this? You would think it would literally wear itself out. But when I reach a sudden plateau in my emotions, just as suddenly I will plunge even deeper.

In recent years, many Americans have spoken publicly of their own experiences with the beast we blithely call "clinical depression." Among them, Mike Wallace of "60 Minutes," William Styron (Pulitzer Prize-winning author of *Sophie's Choice* and other novels), Patty Duke (Oscar-winning actress), Dick Cavett (one of the talk show hosts who did battle with Johnny Carson and lost), Rod Steiger (Oscar-winning actor), Dom DeLuise (comedian and famous chef), and Salvador Loria (who won the Nobel Prize for his work in bacterial genetics).

Among creative artists, writers, and poets, depression has struck even more harshly, leading the following famed personages to suicide: Vincent Van Gogh, Mark Rothko, Robert Lowell, Virginia Woolf, Cesare Pavese, William Inge, Anne Sexton, John Berryman, Randall Jarrell, Sylvia Plath, Hart Crane, Jack London, and Ernest Hemingway, to name only a few. Others, including George Frideric Handel and Gustav Mahler (both famed composers) and Isaac Newton, Winston Churchill, and Franz Kafka suffered severe depressions but managed to turn their psychic energies to their benefit without resorting to self-destruction.

Christians have not been silent on the matter, either. A smattering of books have appeared in the last few years detailing the problem, with many personal case histories provided. Go to a Christian bookstore and you will find books galore on everything from stress and depression to even more focused tomes on mid-life crisis, or recovery from divorce, codependency, or dysfunctional families.

Among Christians, however, there is still a sense of stigma. We are supposed to live "the abundant life" and produce the fruit of the Spirit—"love, joy, and peace" above all. Many do not understand how a committed believer can be so depressed that he cannot function. Above all, how can a good, loving, and all-powerful God allow a Christian to sink into such despair that he takes his own life?

Humanly speaking, no one can answer that question to everyone's satisfaction. We will see part of the answer to that question in the next chapter. God gives us all the power to make choices, and some Christians make the bad choice of taking their own lives. Just as a good and loving God does not prevent Christians from committing other terrible sins, why should we make an exception and take away a Christian's ability to choose to take his own life? Still, we all want to believe that there is a better way to solve the problem than suicide. But it happens.

CHRISTIAN SUPERFICIALITY

I've included this chapter because the dark night experience of intense suffering and pain often involves real, deep, and sometimes debilitating depression. The depression may be the result of loss—the death of a loved one, a firing, a mid-life crisis (loss of youth and dreams)—or for other reasons, such as biochemistry gone awry, illness, or a physical accident (such as Joni Eareckson Tada's paralysis). I reiterate that this book is not a manual for the depressed, and if you are depressed I will not offer a full spectrum look at that subject. However, since real suffering can lead to anxiety, fear, inner doubt, and disillusionment, depression is often the result. It is appropriate to consider the subject in this format as a way of helping those who are broken in the pit of pain.

It dismays me that so many Christian leaders, writers, and preachers are so profoundly unsympathetic to Christians who are depressed. Reverend Don Baker, in his book *Depression*, confesses that his own experience with the illness was exacerbated by the callous attitude he saw in a number of writers:

> I remembered reading Martyn Lloyd-Jones's statement regarding depression. "In a sense a depressed person is a contradiction in terms, and he is a very poor recommendation for the gospel."
>
> Bob George, director of Discipleship Counseling Services in Dallas, Texas, has stated in a Christian periodical, "As children of God, we don't need to be depressed or defeated in life. God has provided us with everything we need for a life of godliness." He went on to say, "When a believer is not experiencing freedom and joy in the Spirit . . . it can only be that he is nearsighted and blind and has forgotten that he has been cleansed from his past sins (2 Pet. 1:9). He has forgotten his position in Christ."
>
> Tim LaHaye states in his book that the primary cause of

depression is self-pity. Others have flatly stated that depression is a sin.

To be forced to acknowledge that I was depressed was, to say the least, depressing.

I hated the word. It was tantamount to sin. My limited knowledge of its meaning and its universality compounded my gloom with guilt and my frustration with anger.[1]

During my own depression, I encountered several such authors and came away convinced they had no idea whereof they spoke. Their forceful and authoritative-sounding declarations have won them a wide audience. But what I read struck me not only as insensitive and self-righteous, but most of all as naive and impossible to practice in the life of a deeply depressed person who may be plunged into a classic dark night of the soul.

It all leads me to a firmer belief in the fact that so many authors come at such suffering as a "thing to get out of" as quickly as possible. It's a sin or a weakness, certainly not something any self-respecting Christian should have to go through. This attitude does not say much for the "plan of God," his sovereignty, or his ability to bring good out of trouble.

Nor does it reckon with reality. Committed Christians sometimes fall into deep inner spiritual darkness. If Jesus himself could utter the ultimate cry of the despondent soul, "My God, my God, why hast thou forsaken me?" who are we to think it should not—cannot—happen to us?

THE EXPERIENCE OF THE DARK NIGHT

Clinical depression is so much a part of the dark-night experience that one is pressed to understand what it is that defines it. In many ways, I suspect that what St. John of the Cross spoke of was, in fact, a deep, clinical depression God used to work in him spiritually.

As I talked with Howard Baker, he remarked, "I would suggest that there are several things that are common to suffering and the classic dark night of the soul. For one thing, a dark night can often be sudden and as if out of nowhere. There would be no logical reasons to point to.

"Second, our therapeutic culture tends to attribute everything to psychological causes rather than spiritual. But I believe there's a rhythm in the spiritual life—the consolation/desolation idea—and God will inevitably bring a growing Christian to a point of testing. It's all through the Bible."

STAGES OF THE CHRISTIAN LIFE

In particular, Baker sees several stages in Christian growth.

1. Conversion
2. Discipleship; tremendous learning and growth
3. Ministry—where you actually serve and produce things for God
4. A time of failure and crisis that precipitates real disillusionment with the idea of ministry as purely "production." This leads to an "inner journey" that moves toward stage five
5. The search for God within—here the disillusioned Christian begins truly to find out who he is in Christ. He seeks God in the experience of everyday life. He wants more intimacy with God and Christ, and he begins to truly enjoy the relationship. He starts practicing new (though classical) disciplines of contemplative prayer (more of a listening form of prayer than speaking), deeper personal prayer, and spiritual reading (reading of Scripture to listen for the voice of God, not just to gain insights and knowledge).

   It's at this point that the sixth stage may come into effect:
6. God removes the consciousness of his presence so that the seeker goes through an intense period of trial, which could be called a "dark night of the soul." God's purpose is to purge the

seeker of sin on a deeper level, bring him into even greater intimacy, and possibly allow God to give him much greater responsibility for "his sheep."

This leads to:

7. Greater and more joyful union with God in ways the seeker
cannot imagine until he has gone through stage six above.

Reverend Baker said, "You can't see this as linear. God will mix
it up to some degree. There may be a lot of stepping back and forward, starts and stops. You may go through the process several
times in a lifetime."

Dr. Bruce Demarest, a professor of systematic theology at Denver Seminary, has conducted a lifelong study of Christian spirituality and the classical disciplines. He calls the dark night a
"deliberate provident withdrawal from the Christian's consciousness to accelerate him in growth and maturity." He sees the
Christian life as having different but clear stages similar to Baker's
model above. Isn't this precisely what C. S. Lewis spoke of as the
"troughs" of Christian life, and the same thing that others have
experienced in terms of divine abandonment?

During my two previous years in seminary, before I slipped
into deep depression, I prayed frequently—probably daily—
"Lord, I want to know you as much as you can possibly be
known by a human being." Though I had no idea this could lead
to the dark night I experienced—and I suspect if I had, I might
not have prayed it!—that was my heart's prayer.

Should I Seek Help?

The more important question for the believer who is convinced he is suffering from clinical depression akin to a true dark
night experience is this: Should he seek medical help?

My response is an unequivocal yes. In any case of intense suffering and especially serious depression, God has allowed biochemi-

cal and background conditions to produce the result. If you have cancer, you pursue all medical means to kill it. Going through the process is all part of the dark night pain that God is using to mature us. By no means would an ill person wait till "the cancer goes away." God does not normally work miracles, no matter how convinced we are that he will in our case.

Moreover, God undoubtedly intends for the believer to be restored through medical attention. Much suffering is so terrible that thoughts of despair can easily drive a person to contemplate suicide—as happened in the case of many people with whom I spoke. That situation is dangerous, and one should not toy with it. The Christian who thinks he is experiencing a "divine abandonment" and shouldn't seek help is putting himself or herself in danger. In fact, St. John of the Cross wrote his book to guide young monks through the experience and to prevent them from total despair of life. More than thirty thousand Americans commit suicide each year, and nearly half or more of them were depressed at the time of their deaths. That is enough to convince me—for I was suicidal for the whole two and a half years (though I never actually attempted it)—that medical help should be sought.

Even with medical help, though, medication is not always the answer. Statistically, psychiatrists admit that many depressions will last an average of six months with or without medication. All medication can do in many cases is provide a modicum of relief until the body heals itself.

SPECIFIC STEPS

If you are experiencing depression that proceeds from what you are sure is a sense of divine abandonment initiated by God himself, consider these steps as a means to ascertain the nature of your depression:

1. Seek the counsel of a doctor to determine whether something physical is wrong. If this is the case, medical help is absolutely necessary. Depression can result from a multitude of causes, including hormonal imbalances, disease, life changes, or grief over a loss. Get a complete physical before taking any other steps. Listen to your doctor's recommendations.

2. Seek the counsel of a psychiatrist who can explain the medical reasons for depression, will give you a competent diagnosis and prognosis, and can recommend a plan of treatment.

3. Seek the counsel of a knowledgeable pastor or spiritual mentor, and discuss your convictions concerning the means of growth and the classic dark night of the soul. Take inventory and examine yourself about the possible sin in your life. Pray together and be accountable to this person. Above all, do not try to "tough this out" on your own without some objective insight into possible causes.

4. If you are severely tempted to suicide, you should take immediate steps to get help. God does not lead anyone to kill themselves. Suicide can be a spontaneous and impulsive act. Many people take that step in the midst of terrible pain they believe they cannot endure, even though it will certainly subside in hours if not minutes. Therefore, if you have feelings of suicide, however slight, do not keep any weapons available, do not allow yourself to spend long periods alone, and above all, get help immediately.

In the end, though, God can and will use even deep depression for good in your life. He will also lead you out of it, even though, while you steep in it, there will be times when you will believe it will never end.

I must encourage you at this point to realize that the dark night of the soul—as manifested by depression or any other form of inner wrangling, anxiety, and pain—has redemptive value. God is doing something, though you may not know what or why. Even today, fifteen years after my own battle, new insights come to my mind every week. I expect that this defining point of my own life will yield purposes that I don't see today but will discover in the years ahead. God never wastes suffering. God in his wisdom, love, and grace uses even pain for good beyond all "that we can ask or think."

In an article in *Christianity Today* on saints suffering in Russia before the Gorbachev revolution, several believers spoke of how suffering in God's design raised and heightened their spiritual priorities and perceptions. One young man described how his persecutions brought him closer to Christ. "When I was persecuted for my faith, I realized that in reality it was Christ who was being persecuted, and with this realization I experienced the presence of Christ in a new way, helping me endure my sufferings."[2]

Anatoli Levitin, a Russian Orthodox layman who was imprisoned for his Christian work, told how his prayer life was raised to new levels through his dark experience: "I felt at ease and well in prison and I left it, strange as it may seem, with stronger nerves, although I had been subjected to very bad conditions the whole time. I would be terribly ungrateful if I did not say to what I owed my feeling of well-being. Here I have only one word: prayer."[3]

While the depression caused by suffering and anxiety from the dark night pressing in upon us can make us feel as if God has vanished, he is just as surely there working to help even before we pray. During an intense period of suffering in 1871, Charles Spurgeon related how he wrestled with the Lord in prayer.

I have found it a blessed thing . . . to plead before God that I am his child. When, some months ago, I was racked with pain to an extreme degree, so that I could no longer bear it without crying out, I asked all to go from the room, and leave me alone; and then I had nothing I could say to God but this, "Thou art my Father, and I am thy child; and thou, as a Father, art tender and full of mercy. I could not bear to see my child suffer as thou makest me suffer; and if I saw him tormented as I am now, I would do what I could to help him and put my arms under him to sustain him. Wilt thou hide thy face from me, my Father? Wilt thou still lay on me thy heavy hand, and not give me a smile from thy countenance?" I talked to the Lord as Luther would have done, and pleaded his fatherhood in real earnest. . . . I bless God that ease came, and the racking pain never returned.[4]

If you are severely depressed and wading through the murk of inexplicable suffering, keep this one thought in mind: God can and will use this for good in your life. He will teach you of prayer and patience and goodness and a hope that can never be broken.

Tell yourself this over and over: "God can and will use this for good in my life." You won't believe it at times. You will hate the idea, and at times the author of it. Your mind will rationalize it, argue against it, shout you down. But be steadfast and believe it. God is working. He will not waste even this. He will redeem it and out of it bring benefits that you will rejoice to see.

Endnotes

1. Don Baker and Emery Nester, *Depression* (Portland, Oreg.: Multnomah Press, 1983), 17.

2. Peter and Anita Deyneka, "Salvation of Suffering: The Church in the Soviet Union, *Christianity Today,* 16 July 1982, 19-21.

3. Ibid.

4. Charles Spurgeon, *Autobiography: The Full Harvest, 1861–1892,* vol. 2 (Carlisle, Pa.: Banner of Truth), 197.

The Fall and Suffering

When Adam and Eve ate the fruit of the tree that gave knowledge of good and evil, they had no idea with what terrible forces they were tampering. That act would plunge the whole world into ruin, a wasteland so terrible and far-reaching that humanity would become a race of criminals whose malice, hatreds, and evil perpetrations would be ended only by the grace and power of God himself.

Why do people suffer?

For a simple reason: because in Adam and Eve we all chose (according to Romans 5:12) to go our own way, to reject God, to be disloyal to him, and to follow a route no one could plan or know, but a route guided by remorseless inner forces desiring only to satisfy oneself. That self had become, in the Fall, a horrifying panoply of illicit and murderous desires. We know the results. They can be characterized by the various kingdoms and leaders of human history: Egypt, with all its idolatry; Babylon and Nineveh, strong in their brutal legions; Rome, with its enslaving armies; Attila the Hun and all his bloodthirsty thousands; the Dark Ages and the Inquisition; the French Revolution and its guillotine; the American Civil War; World War I and the trenches; the Russian Revolution, Marx, Lenin, and Stalin; Hitler and the Holocaust; Pol Pot; Idi Amin; and today, the Ayatollah Khomeini, Qaddafi, and Saddam Hussein.

If suffering could be summarized in a few words, it would start with man's failure in the Garden of Eden. However one decides to parcel out the blame—whether Adam and Eve acted as our agents and therefore our representatives, or whether they acted alone and we must accept the consequences—matters little. God chose to give us one opportunity. We failed. The whole world became disciples of the devil.

WHAT WAS GOD TO DO?

To get a fix on the real problem, though, we have to go back before the Fall, when a being named Lucifer chose to rebel against God. Lucifer, as God's highest and greatest creation, became Satan, the devil, the prince of darkness, the accuser and deceiver of mankind. He was wise and perfect in form, according to Ezekiel 28. But he became proud, perhaps because of all the adulation he received from God's lesser creations (the angels), or perhaps for other reasons. We don't really know.

What is important is that sometime during his reign as archangel, Lucifer decided he wanted more—a higher position, greater power, the throne itself. He wanted to be worshiped, something God would not share. Lucifer, desiring that position of power and honor, persuaded a third of all the angels to join him in a rebellion (see Rev. 12:4). All-out war was declared. Heaven was thrown into turmoil. It appeared God had lost control.

What was God to do with this murderous pretender to the throne and all his rebels? Undoubtedly, God had tried to persuade Lucifer not to rebel, giving him many dire warnings and explicit statements of the consequences of his actions. But Lucifer would hear none of it. So God allowed the rebellion to take place.

Why didn't God stop Lucifer?

There are several reasons. One is that Lucifer, being a volitional creature, had the right to choose to obey or disobey God. It is part of being in God's image. Without a real will and the right to make moral decisions, a creature ceases to be a worthy example of God's person. He becomes a robot. God did not want robots; he wanted moving pictures of himself. God would not create a volitional creature and then demand that it do his bidding; to do so would be to create robots. He wanted real love. To get it, he had to make loving creatures. And that meant the freedom to choose to love or not. Lucifer chose not to.

Another reason God did not stop Lucifer was because he would end up becoming the very thing Lucifer accused him of being: a tyrant, who either got what he wanted or he destroyed you! God could have stopped Lucifer from the start. But what would he do with the remaining angels? Would they now love him purely and perfectly as he desired? Or would they more than likely cringe in terror at his power and demands, becoming obsequious servants who did as they were asked only out of fear of being eliminated?

God did not want such creatures as his chosen. He wanted real worshipers and beloved friends. Above all, he wanted genuine worshipers. To get them, he could not brutally annihilate the rebels; rather, he had somehow to prove to the remaining billions that he was indeed worthy of their love and loyalty.

WHAT GOD DID

So God chose a third course: He let Lucifer and his hordes live on. He gave them certain limited areas of sovereignty. And he allowed them their own rankings and groupings.

Next, he started the grand enterprise: earth. There he would allow Satan and his cohorts to play out their plans, to try their "better" way, and to show all of creation how much more worthy—if they were that—they were than God.

Thus, God created the world and humankind as the testing ground for two basic theories concerning who was most worthy of worship, love, and loyalty—God or Satan. Each was saying, in effect, "Follow me and I will show you glory." Through the experiment of humanity, both God and Satan would show how they treated people, how they ruled, how they guided and loved and led. Satan would be given free rein to try out his theories and show how well he could run the universe, though within the limits of God's goodness and decency. That is, God would not allow Satan to inflict unlimited pain on people or to decimate the planet if a sudden fit of fury came upon him. God would allow him a realistic measure of power to show the "wisdom" of his ways, gradually giving him more freedom up to the end, when he will wield the greatest swathe of power ever.

At the same time, God would work in the world and through his people and followers to demonstrate his purposes and person. He would take the evil Satan inflicted and turn it for good in the lives of the saints. He would lift his chosen above the norm and employ them as resplendent pictures of his own patience, goodness, gentleness, wisdom, and love. At the end there would be an accounting, and all creation would see clearly who was the worthy leader, Lord, and God.

Are We in a Test Tube?

Does this mean we are merely the result of a divine experiment or contest between God and Satan?

Only partly. True, God is employing us to show "through the church, the manifold wisdom of God" and to make it known "to the rulers and authorities in the heavenly realms" (Eph. 3:10). At this very moment, God is demonstrating how wise and good he is through us, the church.

But God has other even greater purposes. Being the ultimate redeemer, he intends far more than simply to terminate rebellion forever, although that is certainly an important goal. Nonetheless, he reserves for humanity the greatest accolade and position we can hope for. We are to "be to the praise of his glory." We are headed for a reign in heaven throughout all the ages. Whenever God wants someone to understand what he is like, he will point to us.

And there is an even greater purpose. It is summed up in the words of the first question of the Westminster Shorter Catechism: "What is the chief end of man? . . . to glorify God and to enjoy him forever."

God's ultimate goal is love, fellowship, friendship, and a dynamic family intimacy that will last forever. Dealing with Satan and his cohorts is only a small part of it. God is capable of far more creative leadership than that. So the idea that we are being employed to show to the angels that God is worthy of their love is just a small portion of his ultimate plan. In humanity, God has made us his brothers and sisters, friends and lovers, something he has not even accorded to angels. We will sit with him on his throne. We will judge the world and those very angels.

Above all, in Christ he became one of us. He entered that sphere of war and suffering, took all its pain and penalty upon himself, and extinguished it forever. He was not a bystander, looking upon us as with a microscope and performing perverse tests and experiments. No, he came down among us and experienced what we experience and then took it all to the limit.

In the movie *The Hiding Place,* a scene in the Ravensbruck camp involves Corrie ten Boom and her sister, Betsie. In the barracks, under degrading conditions with threadbare coverings and lice-ridden beds, the women, cold and hungry, gather around

Corrie and Betsie as they read Scripture to the small group. One of the women calls out with derision, "If your God is such a good God, why does he allow this kind of suffering?" She rips off the bandages on her hands and says, "I'm the first violinist of the symphony orchestra. Did your God will this?"

Corrie, after thought and no little hesitation, finally answers, "We can't answer that question. All we know is that our God came to this earth, and became one of us, and he suffered with us and was crucified and died. And that he did for love."

It would be easy to sling insults at God if he simply remained up there in his heavens, giving orders from his throne like an ivory-tower monarch. But he did not take that kind of stance. He chose to come among us, take our own form, live like us, and then die for us so we might come to his heaven and live with him forever.

How Does This Relate to the Dark Night of Suffering and Pain?

This question, of course, is paramount. But in reality the answer is not difficult. When we realize that on one level we are in a spiritual test tube where an all-out war is being waged, we can see the probability of pain. In a war, people get hurt, injured, maimed, killed. Terrible things happen. Evil runs rampant. Sin erupts moment by moment. Everything takes a greater, more debilitating effort. Nothing comes easy. Everything costs every-thing. War is hell, and though we are not in hell, we are in a hell-ish, dog-kill-dog warfare on all levels.

That may not be particularly consoling to some. Those who lived through a world war or Korea or Vietnam or any of the other twenty or so wars going on in the world at this time know how horrible and brutal war is. They do not wish to go through it but to escape it.

But this spiritual war is inescapable. It is right down inside our own hearts and minds. While there may be a rather fragile "peace among men" as there is on occasion in this world, this divine/satanic war still rages on. Satan roams the earth devouring people and fouling the plans of good men. He rages when one human turns to God and begins following him. He kicks and frets when others think about it. And when he can, he personally attacks those who get in his way.

We suffer because we are in a war.

A Russian Orthodox priest named Dmitri Dudko preached to great crowds in Russia in the early eighties, before the Gorbachev revolution and the dissolution of communism. One of his most appreciated methods was teaching in a forum where the congregants could ask questions. On one occasion when a parishioner asked why there was adversity in the Christian life, Dudko answered, "You still haven't understood the main thing: that our earthly life has been given to us for ascetical struggles; that in our earthly life a battle rages. The devil fights against God, and the field of battle is man's heart, as Dostoyevski said. The Christian is not called a warrior for nothing. His battle ribbons and so forth are in the Kingdom of God."

In 1980, Dudko was imprisoned, questioned, and drugged. He was coerced to make a television confession and recantation of his views. He later wrote, "My personal situation at present is this: I am in the battlefield."[1]

Believers in parts of the world where outward strife far exceeds anything inward understand this warfare better than Americans, who have so much freedom and plenty. We see suffering as a sign of God's disfavor and rejection. However, Russian Christians view it as a sign of God's favor and an indication of God's trust and confidence in his people. Those Russian Christians go so far as to say, "In one sense it seems to us that God has selected the church in Eastern Europe for a special assignment—suffering. Knowing this, of course, does not mean that our sufferings are not agonizing. But it does provide healing and redemption in our suffering."

For them, the conviction is strong: God has sent these sufferings for a purpose, and he will see them through to achieve that purpose. This is a war!

NOT THE END

The idea that we are in a war moves some to laugh, others to scorn, and still others to shake their heads in disbelief. It is a "pessimistic viewpoint" that we should banish from our consciousness. Instead, we should think of mankind as advancing, growing, becoming better able to solve our problems.

But that is something Satan will not allow and therefore God can't bring about now. Why should God let us believe a lie? He will make us see evil for what it is—so that in the end we will never choose evil again. Thus, he sends suffering to wake us up, as C. S. Lewis said, and to engage us in the combat that ever swirls about us.

Still, the idea of a universal all-out war is stultifying, a hopeless view of life—is it not? If that is the end of it, there would truly be little reason for any of us to fight on.

But God has not left us without hope. For one thing, he assures us that he does not allow Satan free reign over anyone. He limits Satan's activities. As he did with Job, he builds a hedge around each of his children. Satan must plead with God for a right to attack (as he did with Peter in Luke 22:31-34, Jesus in Matthew 4:1-11, and Job in Job 1–2). God is always "greater" than "he who is in the world." And Christ has "overcome the world" so that we can experience true joy even in the midst of this war.

It is not as if God has left us without resources or weapons, either. Scripture is full of truth, counsel, and wisdom about the nature of this combat and how to cope in the midst of it. We have spiritual armor, as Paul says to the Ephesians. We battle with spiritual weapons against the arrows of darkness (2 Cor. 10:5-6). And the whole Bible is a battle manual gauged for our spiritual success.

Moreover, God has revealed that the war has already been won. Scripture shows us the "end from the beginning." Satan was defeated at the Cross, and the war goes on only because Christ has not yet returned. Satan fights on because he refuses to accept God's judgment, and God has chosen to wait until all "come to repentance," as Peter says (2 Pet. 3:9) before he eliminates Satan once and for all. When Christ does return, Satan will be chained in hell for a thousand years, and ultimately forever. Every rebel angel will be judged. Every person who has rejected the truth will face God's penalty. And all those who have aligned with Christ will reign.

Thus, the outcome has never been in doubt and never will be. God assures us of that in Scripture. As Georgi Vins, the dissident Russian Baptist pastor, says, "With Christ's help, the church in the East is invincible in spite of all its enemies." And Dmitri Dudko says, "We have nothing to fear since all is ultimately in God's hands."[2]

In 1981, a missionary named Chester Bitterman was murdered in Latin America. His mother, interviewed about her son, commented, "Since we committed Chester to the Lord, we knew whatever the outcome, it would be the Lord's will. We are not to judge. We have seen some encouraging things already from this. We had committed Chet to the Lord's care a long time ago. We are willing to accept this as his will. The Lord doesn't make mistakes."[3]

That is a biblical outlook. It can only proceed from an understanding of the nature of our world as a battleground and the nature of our God as a victorious general who sends his soldiers into battle with no promise but "I will be with you" and "I will bring you safely to my heavenly kingdom."

THE WAY OF ESCAPE

Beyond all this, God has provided us all with a way to escape the madness of war and hell: through faith in Christ. Anyone who will turn to him in faith is promised a home in a new world, where there is no evil. God assures us, "This is not the end. No matter how bad it looks, no matter how bad you feel, it will not always be like this. You are my child, and you will live with me in heaven forever."

Those statements sometimes ring as platitudes. We want something deeper, something more profound. But think about it. Suppose at the beginning of Desert Storm or World War II, God himself had said to us, "I know it looks bad. The enemy appears formidable. But I assure you, he is already defeated. I have put within you all the resources to triumph. I have arranged it so that he will lose—no matter what. All you have to do is get out there and fight."

What of casualties? Perhaps he would say, "I also know you are worried and fearful about your loved ones. It is true that some of your friends and beloved ones will die. In fact, all humankind will face death. But I guarantee, on my life, death is not the end. Rather, it is a doorway to the future world, to heaven. All of us will be reunited again in a better place, a place where there will never be war again."

FAITH THAT OPENS EYES

When Adam and Eve fell, planet earth became a battlefield. The armies continue to gather even after millenniums of conflict, and the forces fight on. People live and die, some never even understanding that this spiritual war is going on. Many struggle with the issue of evil and come up with different, even bizarre answers. Because the war is spiritual, we don't "see" it the way we see real warfare. The idea of a spiritual holocaust seems distant, unreal, even unlikely.

Through faith, though, we become aware of the war and enter into it. As we read Scripture, we learn of all the weapons, deceptions, and devices of this warfare. And in the end, by faith, we see where God is taking it all. By faith we know that no matter how dark it looks, God's day is coming. And if we belong to him, we will be part of that day.

Moment by moment, Jesus cries out in our hearts and through the words of Scripture, "Do not despair. Your pain will pass. My time is coming, and you will on that day be revealed with me in glory. Don't give up. Believe, and hope. You are mine. You will be with me forever. I will not let you down!"

That is profound hope, the kind of hope that Douglas MacArthur must have inspired in his men in the Philippines when he said, "I will return." It is the only real hope to a man or woman in pain. If this world is all we have, if this life is the beginning and end of creation, then pain is a cheat, a thief, a profound enemy we must try to fight, but who will ultimately win every time.

But if pain is just part and parcel of the war, if these wounds are medals, and these scars are badges of triumph and sharing in the sufferings of Christ, then pain is not an enemy who can win. It is only a sure sign that God is working in us and through us. These are the truths we must remind ourselves of when we are in the dark.

These are truths I had to tell myself over and over as I plowed through the pain of depression. They are truths God repeats over and over in Scripture: "I am with you"; "Be anxious for nothing"; "Stand firm"; "Your toil is not in vain in the Lord!"

I have always loved a text in John 6 where Jesus speaks of the hard truths of discipleship. Many disciples found his words insulting. They turned to leave. Jesus looked at the disciples and asked them, "Will you also leave?" Peter answered, "Lord, where else shall we go? You have the words of eternal life."

Through pain those words became cement and iron, and a buttress against the night. We truly have nowhere else to go. But that isn't the end. Jesus has "the words of eternal life."

In the end, the choice for each of us is either to believe or leave. True Christians, though, cannot leave. We indeed have nowhere else to go. So as we struggle against the dark, we find that even the weakest faith, as small as a mustard seed, is an anchor that can hold through the worst storms of our lives. And the light is breaking wide just ahead.

Endnotes
1. Deyneka, *Christianity Today,* 16 July 1982, 19-21.

2. Ibid.

3. "Bitterman—Better Days of Suffering," *Christianity Today,* 10 April 1981, 18.

PART TWO
The Journey

The Disappearance of God

JOURNAL ENTRY— September 19

Why doesn't God answer me? I feel as if he has cut the lines, as if he lopped his person and memory out of my mind. I know he was there once, but now? I feel like I'm banging on the door and no one's home anymore. No, worse, while I turned away to look around the yard, the door did open, and someone put a little sign on the door handle. It says, "Do not disturb, and if you continue disturbing like this, I'll make sure it all gets worse!"

One of the first major sensations of the dark night is abandonment by this God you have come to know as intimate and always near. He seems to disappear from your life and your consciousness. And all hope flees with him.

A pastor I interviewed (who asked to remain anonymous) corroborated this feeling of "a terrible separation from God." He went through a six-month period of deep depression as a result of burnout and stress. He said:

> I believed I was destined for hell. It was so intense I began to think I actually knew what hell was like, even though I knew I was not there. The idea that this could be my eternal state terrified me. It was a sense of deep loneliness, of isolation. It was like I had a knife stuck in my brain, hot with mental anguish.
>
> That is the word: *Anguish*. I never understood it before, even through the loss of relatives and friends. But anguish just poured through me, this wrenching sense of distance from God, as if he hated me and was trying to destroy me. Theologically, I knew that was untrue. But this was not a rational thing. It was an emotion so intense and overwhelming, it would be like trying to stand in the face of tsunami and not lose your balance.

People going through the dark night use strong terminology: Anguish. Tsunami. Utter separation. Total despair. Hell.

God seems to disappear. He is not just distant. Not just far away. Rather, it's as if he no longer exists. You have been cast out into a dark that can be felt, as happened to the Egyptians during the ten plagues of Moses. All your senses are intact. But the sun has gone out of your life. You don't know when it will come up again.

The disappearance of God is the quintessential experience of the dark night despair—an impelling, overwhelming sense of inner blackness and forsakenness. Go to a doctor and he might prescribe medications like Tofranil, Elavil, Prozac, Stelazine, Navane, Haldol, lithium, Ativan, Mellaril, Thorazine, or Prolixin. But nothing seems to work.

We know all the promises: "I came that they might have life";

"I will give you rest"; "My peace I leave with you." But all those great words are placed in jeopardy. That feeling of joy, hope, and love for everyone is just gone, as if it has been gouged out of you, surgically removed, canceled, ripped away, and shredded. "Peace like a river" is almost a joke. Your mind is out of control with a flood of anxieties, worries, doubts, and hang-ups that no amount of prayer, Bible memory, church attendance, or witnessing can seem to vanquish.

You feel mentally and emotionally obliterated. The promise of Hebrews 13:5 (NASB), "I will never desert you, nor will I ever forsake you," mocks you. The passage in Psalm 46:1 (NASB), "God is our refuge and strength, a very present help in trouble," would be laughable if the inner pain weren't so great. "God a present help! Ha!"

You start to become a cynic. You are always "down," always struggling, ever and always groping for an answer. But it doesn't seem to come.

A DIFFERENT KIND OF DISCOVERY

At the same time, you start to discover other texts, which, astonishing to you, seem to speak directly to your situation:

> As the deer pants for the water brooks, so my soul pants for Thee, O God. My soul thirsts for God, the living God; when shall I come and appear before God? My tears have been my food day and night, while *they* say to me all day long, "Where is your God?" (Ps. 42:1-3, NASB)
>
> O LORD, rebuke me not in Thy wrath; and chasten me not in Thy burning anger. For Thine arrows have sunk deep into me, and Thy hand has pressed down on me. There is no soundness in my flesh because of Thine indignation; there is no health in my bones because of my sin. (Ps. 38:1-3, NASB)

William Styron recently described the feelings of his own dark night in his book *Darkness Visible* as a "veritable howling tempest in the brain."

Charles Spurgeon, the nineteenth century "prince of preachers" in London's Metropolitan Tabernacle, spoke of such periods as "extremes of wretchedness."

John Bunyan gave it a place: The Slough of Despond.

Martin Luther referred to it as "heaviness of mind and melancholy."

C. S. Lewis would describe it this way in his book *A Grief Observed:*

> Meanwhile, where is God? This is one of the most disquieting symptoms. When you are happy, so happy that you have no sense of needing Him, so happy that you are tempted to feel His claims upon you as an interruption, if you remember yourself and turn to Him with gratitude and praise, you will be—or so it feels—welcomed with open arms. But go to Him when your need is desperate, when all other help is vain, and what do you find? A door slammed in your face, and a sound of bolting and double bolting on the inside. After that, silence. You may as well turn away. The longer you wait, the more emphatic the silence will become. There are no lights in the windows. It might be an empty house. Was it ever inhabited? It seemed so once. And that seeming was as strong as this. What can this mean? Why is He so present a commander in our time of prosperity and so very absent a help in time of trouble?[1]

What makes it worse is that other Christians seem to be like they were before. God is there. Why, he just answered this prayer last week! But toward you this God has imposed a vow of silence. It feels like a personal vendetta.

You go to the Bible and what do you find—someone like King Saul, to whom God has sent a demon to hound and afflict as a punishment for his mistake of disobedience. Or else you note how God banished Moses from the "land of milk and honey" because he struck the stone twice in anger.

Those two cases are enough to fill you with dread. But then there's Job, caught in the crossfire between God and Satan. Next, you discover Hosea, who was forced to wed a harlot and then stick by her even though she rejected him over and over. There is Jonah, who, despite some ingrained and somewhat understandable prejudices, ended up in the belly of a fish pleading for his life. Or take Abraham, who was promised a son and then had to wait twenty-five years before his ninety-year-old wife got pregnant.

All these events and more blast the ever-ready-to-question mind of the dark night sojourner. We've all heard God is mysterious. But to the disillusioned person, assaulted by his own dark images of pain and hell, God's nature is turned on end. He ceases to be gracious, kind, compassionate. Even his holiness, justice, and righteousness become caricatures. In its place is a monster who conjures up images of the Nazi medical practitioners. I found myself asking, "If God can *let* this kind of pain happen to me, what else will he *let* happen to me?"

Still, all your friends are fine. They know God's still there. They are not worried or in the slightest agony of soul. "What's the problem?" they query. "Look around! God is giving us a happy and meaningful life!"

So you come to another conclusion: God has not vanished. No, something else has happened: He has personally rejected you. He hates you!

And that is only the beginning.

BUT IS IT TRUE?

Lest this gloom and doom become unreadable, let's ask a rhetorical question: Has God truly disappeared?

Consider just for a moment the immensity of the idea. Because someone personally feels abandoned and alone, the omnipotent God has disappeared from the universe. Is that possible?

Of course not. But it is this feeling inside you that is so real, so overpowering. It is the same thing Job felt as he sat on his ash heap and asked, "Why has God left me here like this?" The disciples had the experience in the boat during the storm, when they were about to sink. "Save us, Lord," they cried. "We are perishing." They felt as if God had blinked or had fallen asleep!

This sensation of God's disappearance is troubling and difficult to get beyond. But what has really happened? God has withdrawn the "sense of his presence" from our conscious perception. The combination of these sensations of despair and rejection leads to a deeper feeling of solitude, of being utterly alone.

Yet, in the midst of it all, you find something else: You cannot cease to believe. A vestige of faith is rooted in you, and it won't let go.

Sheldon Vanauken, whose story of the life and death of his wife in *A Severe Mercy*, ranks as an epic of God's goodness in the midst of agonizing personal turmoil. As he traveled the lonely path of grief following the death of his wife, Davy, he wrote:

> God seemed remote. The world was still empty without Davy, and now God seemed to have withdrawn, too. My sense of desolation increased. God could not be as loving as He was supposed to be, or—the other alternative. One sleepless night, drawing on to morning, I was overwhelmed with a sense of cosmos empty of God as well as Davy. "All right," I muttered to myself. "To hell with God. I'm not going to believe this damned rubbish any more. Lies, all lies. I've been

had." Up I sprang and rushed out to the country. This was the end of God. Ha!

And then I found I *could not* reject God. I could not. I cannot explain this. One discovers one cannot move a boulder by trying with all one's strength to do it. I discovered—without any sudden influx of love or faith—that I could not reject Christianity. Why I don't know. There it was. I could not.[2]

In the dark of deep suffering, there is an intense, overwhelming feeling that God has changed, given up, thrown you away, handed you over to the devil.

And yet you still can't let go of him. Why? Because he has knit that truth deep within you—deeper than your own thoughts. He cannot leave you, forsake you, reject you, or give up on you, even when you despair of him. And deep down, in some mysterious way, we cling to him. Like Job said, "Though he slay me, yet will I trust him."

W. E. Sangster was one of the great Methodist preachers of England in the 1940s and 1950s. He led the church to grow greatly in evangelism, prayer, and personal holiness. His sermons and books awoke many in the British Isles to the power and importance of personal evangelism. He was a flame that would not go out, until in 1957 physical problems slowed him down. Then in 1958, he was diagnosed as having progressive muscular atrophy with both the cause and cure unknown. Sangster struggled, fought an inner battle, and then made four resolutions: "I will never complain. I will keep the home bright. I will count my blessings. I will try to turn it to gain."

A little later he wrote, "There have been great gains already from my sickness. I live in the present. I am grateful for little things. I have more time—and use it—for prayer."

In the end, Sangster could move only two fingers, which he

used to communicate with his family and others. On May 24, 1960, he died. It was Wesley Day, a special day of memorial for the founder of the Methodist church. Undoubtedly, it was a gift Sangster regarded as a special providence. More than fifteen hundred attended his funeral.

At one point it must have looked to Sangster as if God had deserted him at the height of his powers and influence. But he knew it was not so, and he endured because of that truth. God had put it deep inside him, and he didn't even know it was there until God allowed him to suffer.

It is the same for us.

Endnotes

1. C. S. Lewis, *A Grief Observed* (New York: Bantam Books, 1976), 4–5.

2. Sheldon Vanauken, *A Severe Mercy* (New York: Harper and Row Publishers, 1977), 190.

Lists, Arguments, Complaints, and Glimmers of Hope

JOURNAL ENTRY— November 8

Made a list of worries and remedies today to try something new.

1. I am worried I will never get married.

   You're twenty-five years old. What's the sweat? Go out on a date. Get to know some people. John 10:10.
2. I'm worried I might crack up and end up a deadhead in a mental institution.

   All right, so what? You'll be taken care of. Things could be worse.
3. I'm worried I might not do this list right.

   So do it first.

So why am I worried about all these things? Why can't I just shake it? Why doesn't logic, reason, prayer, "talking to myself," or anything else work?

Frequently during my dark night, I found myself making lists. Sometimes they were steps to take to get out of the darkness transfusing my soul. Sometimes they were several new "insights" that had occurred to me. And as in the above list, worry was a persistent problem.

In particular, the feeling that I was destined for hell disturbed me, as it did others I have interviewed. There is an incessant cyclical argument that seems to go through the heads of Christians caught in a dark night. It goes like this:

You feel worthless and useless. You're convinced you're stuck in this condition for the rest of your life, and thus it will be misery upon misery for as long as you live.

Next, you start to think that perhaps you will be miserable not only in this life but in the next, too. Everyone will be enjoying heaven except you and the other sufferers. Even there God will be unable to heal you.

You consider suicide, know it is wrong, and try to tell yourself not to think about that. But the impulse returns again and again.

After this, you begin to suspect that it is possible you are so fouled up as a person that you are not really a Christian after all. So you begin, as many do, to pray that "Christ come into your heart" almost every day. One man felt he must have done something wrong the first time—it didn't take, so he had to pray it again. But the next day (or the next minute), he thought, *I must have left something out. I must have made a mistake.* So he went through the whole process again—to no avail, no relief, and no sense of assurance.

The thoughts get even more stifling: You begin to think that God may not be like the God of the Bible at all. You ask, "What if he just decides to send me to hell anyway? Or what if I die by natural means and get up there and he says, 'You didn't receive Jesus properly while on earth, so it's over, you're done! Bye-bye!'"

Bible passages come to mind: "What if I'm one of those in

Matthew 7 (NASB) who say, 'Lord, Lord, did we not prophesy in Your name, and in Your name cast out demons, and in Your name perform many miracles?' What if he says to me, 'I never knew you, depart from Me!'"

It goes around and around. The thoughts become an inundation, a typhoon of thoughts and impressions whirling around in your head.

It is as if the devil heaves up every internal personal problem with sin, be it pride, envy, jealousy, or covetousness, and he magnifies it and then flings it all back in your face till you must face it times without number. "Do you think God can love you when you're like that?"

THEOLOGICAL PROBLEMS

Often there are also heavy artillery battles inside your mind over various theological truths. For instance, I wrote in my journal:

> I keep thinking about "the sovereignty of God." For three years now I've learned God is in charge, he "works all things for good," and nothing happens that is beyond his reach, power, wisdom, and plan.
> So I ask: Did he cause this to happen to me?
> The answer, I am told, is no, God does not cause evil.
> Then I say, "Has he allowed it for some purpose?"
> Most assuredly.
> "So what is that purpose?"
> I am told I may never know. Job didn't.
> It's all so very comforting.

God's sovereignty is a vast comfort for most Christians. It means nothing ultimately happens in this world that is a fluke or a mistake. Everything can be used by God for good.

But for the person caught on the dark side of pain and suffering, God's sovereignty can also become a glaring affront to logic.
Read that the destruction of Job happened because Satan challenged God to prove a point, and you might come away with
some very ugly ideas about God's true nature. You can find yourself wondering if God might not be a Dr. Mengele!

Something Good

Still, God is working subtly now, unseen, and there is a bal-
ancing truth here: Though the sufferer feels rejected and isolated,
he fights on for answers he believes have to be there. God cannot
have disappeared because he knows too many people and friends
who claim he is there and as sure as ever. He has put within his
child an unwavering (though deep) belief: God has to be doing
something even though I can't see it!

One woman, an ex-police officer, battled the issue of suffering
and evil for months. She had seen so much of the dark side of life
in her profession that it drove her to attempt suicide. She sat
down with her police revolver and began playing Russian rou-
lette. Six times she spun the cylinder, placed the barrel to her
head, and pulled the trigger. Six times there was only a click.

Astonished that she didn't blow her head off, she concluded that
God must love her very much to protect her under those conditions.
Her search for answers led her to return to the faith and a new pro-
fession. But it was only through such darkness that she found light.

I remember my professor, Dr. Howard Hendricks, telling his
class of a visit to India, where a woman held up the stumps of her
leprous hands and said, "I thank God for these hands and this disease, for without them I might not have found Jesus."

God Does Answer

Often, there are respites, oases in the emotional desert that
God allows to cheer his child. The dark is a time of feeling

abjectly forsaken. But the truth is that God can never forsake us
or abandon us, just as the Bible states over and over.

For me, "God with us" was one of the greatest discoveries of
becoming a Christian. For the first time in my life, I felt secure.
There really was nothing to fear. No one was greater than God,
and he was on my side!

In the dark night, though, all that security seems to dissolve. We
suddenly feel as if this person we have trusted has turned against
us. It is as if God himself hates us, has rejected us, and is punishing
us relentlessly through the night.

Why does God let us feel this way? I believe these feelings are
part of learning true trust. It is easy to trust someone close, who
has dynamic words, a powerful presence, tremendous financial
security, or just broad shoulders next to us as we go out in public.
But what happens when all of God's financial and physical muscle
seem to go out the window? What happens when God stops
"doing" anything for us, as when the evangelist loses his mystical
power and no one comes forward again? Where do we turn when
in the face of our enemies all we can do is run, and when we
stand we get mowed down, as those first Christians did under the
Roman persecutions?

But when we look around us—feeling abandoned, alone, over-
whelmed—and still *trust,* we have greatly pleased God. Trusting
him even though everything has gone wrong is real trust, the
kind God is teaching us through the dark night.

Two Great Texts

One of the great texts in all of Scripture is found in
Isaiah 40:27–31. There, God speaks through Isaiah to the scat-
tered millions of Israel. The people looked around and saw
nothing but crumbling walls, burned cities, and enslaved
friends and neighbors. They were undone. There was no more
hope, no joy, nothing.

But what does God say:

Why do you say, O Jacob,
and complain, O Israel,
"My way is hidden from the LORD;
my cause is disregarded by my God"?
Do you not know?
Have you not heard?
The LORD is the everlasting God,
the Creator of the ends of the earth.
He will not grow tired or weary,
and his understanding no one can fathom.
He gives strength to the weary
and increases the power of the weak.
Even youths grow tired and weary,
and young men stumble and fall;
but those who hope in the LORD
will renew their strength.
They will soar on wings like eagles;
they will run and not grow weary,
they will walk and not be faint.

What are these words but an exact picture of real faith? Real faith does not look around and complain, "God no longer cares about me. He doesn't even look on me anymore." No, real faith, even in the face of ultimate destruction, reckons with the truth: God is. Therefore I will hope in him, and he will restore; he will give strength, he will make us walk and run again!

The other passage is Habakkuk 3:17–19. Here is a man who sees all the lechery, dishonesty, greed, murder, and lying of Judah. He doesn't understand why God doesn't do something. So he cries out and God answers: "I am doing something. I'm going to send the Babylonians, and they will wipe out all the evildoers and take everyone else into slavery!"

Habakkuk is plunged into mortal anguish. He questions; he argues; he challenges. But in the end, he sees. His final words are the essence of real faith:

> *Though the fig tree does not bud*
> *and there are no grapes on the vines,*
> *though the olive crop fails*
> *and the fields produce no food,*
> *though there are no sheep in the pen*
> *and no cattle in the stalls,*
> *yet I will rejoice in the LORD,*
> *I will be joyful in God my Savior.*
> *The Sovereign LORD is my strength;*
> *he makes my feet like the feet of a deer,*
> *he enables me to go on the heights.*

What is real faith in God but continuing to believe in the face of everything in life gone wrong? What is true belief and trust in Christ but trusting him and believing his Word even when nothing has worked out? It is easy to believe in him when things are going well. But under such circumstances it is hard to see if the faith is real. How do we know our faith is not just good feelings because of our positive circumstances? Take away the good circumstances and the presence of or lack of real faith will be obvious.

The dark night is meant to produce such faith. It is painful. It is agonizing. But when that kind of faith flowers, nothing can shake it. God is determined to produce that kind of faith in us, and he will settle for nothing less. That is why he does not flinch to use such a terrible tool as intense pain and suffering. The end—glory—is worth the price.

EIGHT

Disheartening Revelations

For the Christian, one of the worst aspects of the dark night is the fact that our faith is so assaulted by what we are feeling. Prayer seems not only to be left unanswered, but hurled back at us with livid recriminations. "Who are you to challenge me? Who are you to question my wisdom?!" Like the professor controlling the Great Oz in the movie, the great one repeatedly fends off Dorothy's requests as audacious and arrogant. "I am the Great Oz! Now, gooooooo!" In fact, if we read Job 38–42, that is almost how God seems to respond to Job.

How Long, O Lord?

Above it all, the question When will it end? roars inside us like a great wounded beast. We are sure that if God would just tell us how much longer we have to hang in there, we could survive.

Dr. Viktor Frankl observed this problem in the concentration camps during the time when he was an inmate. He wrote in his renowned study of that experience, *Man's Search for Meaning:*

> Former prisoners, when writing or relating their experiences, agree that the most depressing influence of all was that a prisoner could not know how long his term of imprisonment would be. He had been given no date for his release. . . .
>
> A well-known research psychologist has pointed out that life in a concentration camp could be called a "provisional existence." We can add to this by defining it as a "provisional existence of unknown limit." . . .
>
> A man who could not see the end of his "provisional existence" was not able to aim at an ultimate goal in life. He ceased living for the future, in contrast to a man in normal life. Therefore, the whole structure of his inner life changed; signs of decay set in which we know from other areas of life. The unemployed worker, for example, is in a similar position.[1]

That kind of uncertainty nags at the sufferer and lays him even lower. If there was just the surety of a cure, of change, of hope. The person asks, "Why can't I just get back to normal again? Should that be so hard for God—if he loves me? Is that such a selfish, foolish, arrogant request? After all, he said, 'Ask and you shall receive' and 'Come to me you who are weary and heavy-laden, and I will give you rest.' I'm weary, and God knows I'm heavy-laden. I just want rest. Why does he withhold it? Am I being overbearing with him? Demanding? Inconsiderate? Have I offended him?"

He begins confessing every sin he can think of, hoping that through confession he will be set free.

THE FORMULA MYTH
As the pressures mount, he digs in, searching for an answer—perhaps a formula that will knock him out of this emotional

maelstrom. It is then that he often finds that the old formulas don't work.

JOURNAL ENTRY— October 12
Over and over I have told myself to Pray-Believe-Wait. So I explain; I argue; I pray. But nothing changes. My condition is the same as ever.

All the old formulas and the tried-and-tested principles that once worked with such effortless consistency suddenly become impotent before the ravages of the dark night. During that period, I read many books on suffering, evil, depression, and pain. I was searching for some explicit prescription for an exit from my throes. Reluctantly, I must say I found many of the lists, panaceas, and "surefire remedies" unworkable, and some ridiculous.

What was even harder to take was that the Christian writers (in contrast to secular authors) were often the most simplistic and unrealistic. Some had no sympathy, and they were so sure their remedies would work. Often they were extremely critical of the larger psychiatric and medical establishment. It would anger me to read their victorious-sounding, God-inspired, "scripturally correct" language. None of them that I could find had ever described or experienced darkness like what I was going through, and it was disconcerting for them to blithely offer authoritative answers that I found didn't work, even though I had tried them to the letter.

I'm not saying that what some of these sincere authors wrote didn't work for them. Or that they won't work for anyone else. I'm not even saying they were exaggerating their own success.

But the kind of pain that many sufferers go through often makes such efforts prohibitive. For instance, to simply "thank God" over and over for your circumstances as one author suggested will not automatically make the sufferer feel better. In fact, he might realize he is only using such a "tactic" to manipulate God into giving him what he really wants, which is relief. It becomes a self-defeating exercise.

Another author advised his readers to "praise God" and that there was "real power in praise." I'm sure there is, but many of my praises felt like grit in my mouth. My heart didn't mean or feel any of them.

WHY?

More than anything, I wanted to know why this had happened to me. What had I done wrong? Was I genetically defective? Why couldn't the doctors help me. Was there an answer? Was I asking something no one could answer?

C. S. Lewis has an interesting comment on that issue in his book *A Grief Observed:*

> When I lay these questions before God, I get no answer. But a rather special sort of "No answer." It is not the locked door. It is more like a silent, certainly not uncompassionate, gaze. As though He shook His head not in refusal but waiving the question. Like, "Peace, child; you don't understand."
>
> Can a mortal ask questions which God finds unanswerable? Quite easily, I should think. All nonsense questions are unanswerable. How many hours are there in a mile? Is yellow square or round? Probably half the questions we ask—half our great theological and metaphysical problems—are like that.[2]

An excellent thought. I am convinced that part of this whirlwind of questions has two purposes:

1. To drive us to find answers.
2. To make us realize that some questions have no easy answers.

Thus it may take time, patience, and trust to reach an island of acceptance.

In this respect, Tim Hansel wrote in his journal:

> This is a time of great fatigue and disorientation. If I only knew how long it was going to last. "What I want from you is your true thanks. I want you to trust me in your times of trouble so that I can rescue you and you can give me joy."[3]

Joni Eareckson Tada put it this way in an interview:

> The first months, even years, I was consumed with the unanswered questions of what God was trying to teach me. I probably secretly hoped that by figuring out God's ideas, I could learn my lesson and then he would heal me.[4]

It is the same for many in the dark night. We are convinced if we can only learn what this great lesson is, we will be catapulted out of our pain. But what if there is no such "special lesson" God is trying to teach? What if God has much more in mind than a simple principle, idea, or biblical insight?

THE NEED FOR HOPE

Such questions and feelings cannot be dismissed lightly. One must have hope to survive. He must believe that God, who is somehow behind all this, is leading it all to a grand conclusion. But he must also determine to sift through his questions and decide which ones are truly impossible and which ones he should seek answers for. I struggled for more than a year with questions about the Bible's accuracy, Jesus' deity and resurrection, and God's existence. Studying through the answers anchored my faith more

deeply in "the facts." I didn't feel better. But the truth had
become stitched into my heart.

CONVICTED OF A TERRIBLE SIN, BUT WHICH ONE?
Another nagging issue is the feeling that we must have
sinned horribly to deserve what is happening to us.

JOURNAL ENTRY— November 12
Over and over I confess sins. Old sins assault me, things I confessed long ago and even went to the people concerned to
ask forgiveness. Now my mind screams, "You weren't sincere.
You didn't tell everything. You held back. You never even dealt
with *that one* the way you should have!" How much can I do?
Do I have to fix and refix and re-refix the same wrongs over
and over again? Nothing satisfies this suddenly all-powerful
conscience of mine.

This "confession of sin" is one more symptom of the dark
night. It is a picture of a man racing around panic-stricken, looking for the route of escape. Many times now when I read the
book of Job, I marvel at how often Job challenged God to show
him his sin. He repeatedly questioned God, asked for "an umpire"
to decide, and challenged the Creator to come down and debate
the matter. He wanted to find out what the sin was and be done
with it.

Similarly, the sufferer is often convinced that there must be
some secret error somewhere, which if he could just find it,
would fix everything.

It becomes an endless cycle. Past sins race around in your mind
like the tigers turning to butter in the story of "Little Black
Sambo." Dr. Rick Cornish told me, "At times, it was like those
old cartoons where the dogs are chasing one another's tails and
going faster and faster till it becomes a blur. I would get this train

of thought going around in my mind—that I was doomed, that this misery in my mind and heart would go on and on forever, that I was condemned to hell, that I had no relationship with God, that I had been deluded all along—one thought would lead to the next, all of it going round and round in a whirlwind. It was exhausting, like a literal roaring inside my mind.

"All of this produced and heightened my inner sense of dread and the feeling of being abandoned by God.

"There were moments when the pain and darkness were so intense I thought I might black out or faint. But it was even more tangible than that. I felt in a real sense as if my mind might be obliterated, that it might cease to exist."

ASSURANCE

Thus, the dark night is infused with the thought and question: Does God still love me? Is this inner darkness, this feeling of desolation, a sign that he has rejected me forever?

The feeling of having lost the love of God can easily drive a person to despair. I suspect that is precisely what Peter felt when he denied he knew Jesus three times the night of the Lord's arrest. He went out and wept, and perhaps believed that he had suffered a complete dismissal from God's love and care.

But who was one of the first Jesus came to after his resurrection? Peter. God's love for him was so great—even in the face of this embarrassing failure—that he longed to assure Peter that he still loved him and would never let him go.

I honestly think the love of God has gotten plenty of bad press in our day. Some have turned it into a license for sin. Others have traded and bartered on it as if it were a sum of money. Still others hold it out like a carrot to the hopeless, only to pull it back if the person doesn't fulfill all the other so-called requirements of discipleship and Christian living.

I'm not sure how to untangle all the threads of lordship, salvation, and discipleship.

But this I know now—a conviction bred through the experience of the dark night: There is nothing that can separate a Christian from the love of God. Not "trouble or hardship or persecution or famine or nakedness or danger or sword."

There is nothing that can tear us out of God's hands, for as Paul says, "I am convinced that neither death nor life, neither angels nor demons, neither the present nor the future, nor any powers, neither height nor depth, nor anything else in all creation, will be able to separate us from the love of God that is in Christ Jesus our Lord."

If we think this is just Paul's opinion, we can mark Jesus' own words: "My sheep listen to my voice; I know them, and they follow me. I give them eternal life, and they shall never perish; no one can snatch them out of my hand. My Father, who has given them to me, is greater than all; no one can snatch them out of my Father's hand" (John 10:27-29).

God's love is so high and deep and wide and long that it will take us an eternity to understand it. It is one of many certainties we can depend on even when our emotions are screaming with doubt.

If you are experiencing a dark night at this very moment, read the words of Paul in Romans 8 and of Jesus in John 10. Read them over and over. Memorize them. Brand them on your heart and mind. Let God himself speak them into your soul. They are sober truths spoken by our Lord with all the sincerity of his holiness.

Consider it again: There is nothing you can do to lose God's personal love for you.

Nothing.

Ever.

Forever.

Endnotes

1. Viktor E. Frankl, *Man's Search for Meaning* (New York: Pocket Books, 1963), 110–112.

2. C. S. Lewis, *A Grief Observed* (New York: Bantam Books, 1976), 80–81.

3. Tim Hansel, *You Gotta Keep Dancin'* (Elgin, Ill.: David C. Cook, 1985), 33.

4. Philip Yancey, *Where Is God When It Hurts?* (Grand Rapids, Mich.: Zondervan, 1977), 119.

NINE

God's Word No Longer Works

JOURNAL ENTRY— November 21

I latched onto a Scripture, was going to test God, see if he really would come through. It was Philippians 4:6-7 [NASB]: "Be anxious for nothing, but in everything by prayer and supplication with thanksgiving let your requests be made known to God." I followed it precisely. I refused to be anxious. Then I prayed and gave him my requests. I even gave thanks for what was happening and what would happen.

Nothing changed. In fact, as usual, it only got worse.

I did it over and over.

I so desperately want this Scripture to work. I need peace, real peace. But I find that for me it doesn't come.

This is another element of the disquiet of the dark night: Scripture no longer seems to work as it once did so perfectly and effortlessly. I remember a good friend telling me how

God responded to his prayers so quickly: "I had a headache, I prayed about it, and zoom, it was gone."

A boy of nine told us all at the dinner table one night how he'd been out in the school yard flying his kite and there was no wind. So he just said, "Please Lord, send some wind!" And suddenly a breeze whipped up.

Read any number of "how to" books in the Christian bookstore, and you will learn there's "power in praise," "power in positive prayer," "power in thankfulness," and so on.

But for the Christian unable to see a light in the darkness, Scripture often seems closed off to him. Nothing "works" anymore. "Ask and you shall receive" just isn't so! "Come to me and I will give you rest," seems more like a slap in the face. You come—every hour, every minute—but there's no rest in sight or heart.

Dr. Rick Cornish told me of his experience with 1 Corinthians 10:13, the verse that promises in temptation God "will provide the way of escape so that we can endure it." He said, "I felt God had miscalculated. I felt he had pushed me farther than I could endure. My mind kept telling me I was damaged goods. Broken. Useless. I'd never be able to serve him effectively again. He had taken it too far; he had not been faithful, as 1 Corinthians 10:13 said."

WHAT IS A RELATIONSHIP WITH GOD?

This seems to be a perennial question among those living through a dark night: Does God's Word really work? If I apply the truth, will it change my life?

The answer to which God leads us, I believe, is that Scripture is not a vending machine in which we put in money and out pops the product. Scripture, rather, is a dynamic, living entity with the very life of God implanted in its meanings. As Paul wrote to Timothy, it is "useful for teaching, rebuking, correcting and training in righteousness." Part of the "training" and teaching is to discover how to walk with God and learn of him through his Word. That involves interaction, intimacy, relating. Any relationship has its ups and downs. More importantly, a relationship with God involves many kinds of interaction:

wife to husband
servant to master
disciple to teacher
patient to doctor
creature to Creator
lover to lover
lost, dying man to rescuer
dependent to provider
sinner to confessor
worshiper to Almighty
asker to giver
friend to friend
soldier to general
player to coach
picture to artist
sorrower to Comforter
despairer to encourager
questioner to answerer
disobedient to discipliner

At any given time, one or more facets of that relationship may be in effect. Thus, we do not just know God as provider or lover or friend and leave it there. God is always drawing us into other levels of that intimacy. He wants a "rounded" relationship with us, and that calls for many different kinds of interaction.

Dr. Cornish says of his encounter with God over 1 Corinthians 10:13:

I learned that I could endure through far more than I ever thought I could. God had not pushed me too far; he'd only pushed me farther than I thought I could go. It's like running a marathon. Sooner or later you hit what is called "the wall"—usually about twenty miles out. A lot of people who run marathons don't think they'll get through it, because when you hit the wall, you feel that everything is gone mentally and physically. You can't go another step. You just want it to be over.

But somehow you just push on through the blinding pain, and suddenly you find you can make it. You can keep on going. That's in a way what God did with me. He showed me he could take me farther than I'd ever been before. In my mind, that's an achievement worth possessing.

William Barclay gives the illustration of Sir Edward Elgar, the famed composer, who listened to a girl singing a solo from one of his works. The girl was flawless, achieving near perfect tone and clarity. Elgar commented, "She will be truly great when something happens to break her heart."

How true. It is only through pain that we develop heart, soul, passion, and the character that can move people and even nations.

In this respect, the dark night of suffering is much the same as what a coach puts a team through. In order to develop them as players, he wrings them out, pushes them to limits they never thought they could reach, and forces them through exercises that may look formidable to the point of impossibility. If God were only interested in getting us to do and be what we already know we can do and be, then what need would there be for God?

God wants a full-blown relationship that will not only develop us as people in his image, but will also bring us to a place of intimacy with him that is nothing less than complete spiritual fulfillment.

SUFFERING AND RELATING

Hard as it is to accept, suffering is part of relating to him. It is not just training or discipline; it is entering into the "fellowship of His sufferings" (NASB), as Paul put it in Philippians 3. God means for us to so understand and know him that we will love what he loves, hate what he hates, and desire what he desires. That does not mean we are to become clones of him; rather, it means our love and care for each other is so great that we become "one" in heart and soul.

Through relating to God in Christ and through undergoing the transformation necessary to give us a "rounded" relationship with him, we must go through some measure of pain, just as a surgeon must inflict pain to heal. The Fall rendered us hopelessly depraved. Coming to Christ is like invading Normandy. The beginning of the end has started. We are redeemed, reclaimed, marked as "his." But there is still much ground to cover and win back. God is building an eternal kingdom. The here and now is fleeting. Our goals in this world, while important to him because they are important to us, are not his final purpose. He longs that we regain the right perspective. So he puts us into the refinery in order to bring us out as gold.

KEEPING PERSPECTIVE

Thomas Merton, the famed Trappist monk and writer, said this of the Desert Fathers, those fifth- and sixth-century mystics who left the world and sought the reality of God in the desert:

Society was regarded by [the Desert Fathers] as a shipwreck from which each single individual man had to swim for his life. . . . These were men who believed that to let oneself drift along, passively accepting the tenets and values of what they knew as society, was purely and simply a disaster.[1]

While the sufferer asks, "Why don't you take it all away? When will it end? Why is this happening to me?" he should also ask, "Isn't God taking me to heaven? Won't he give me understanding one day? Isn't he wise, loving, and good?"

Viktor Frankl wrote in *Man's Search for Meaning:*

> Once the meaning of suffering had been revealed to us, we refused to minimize or alleviate the camp's tortures by ignoring them or harboring false illusions or entertaining artificial optimism. Suffering had become a task on which we did not want to turn our backs. We had realized its hidden opportunities for achievement. . . . One could make a victory of those experiences, turning life into an inner triumph, or one could ignore the challenge and simply vegetate as did a majority of the prisoners.[2]

Frankl does not write from a Christian perspective, but he speaks a truth that is worth learning: Simply enduring through suffering is an achievement that is worth gaining. The believer doesn't have to work up some ephemeral, sham joy. He doesn't have to smile on the world. But endurance, real steadfastness in spite of difficulty, is a character trait worth obtaining. And one God values greatly.

I like what Eugene Peterson has written on this issue:

> This is not to say joy is a moral requirement for Christian living. Some of us experience things that are full of sadness and pain. Some of us descend to low points in our lives when joy seems to have permanently departed. We must not, in such circumstances or during such times, say, "Well, that's the final proof that I am not a good Christian. Christians are supposed to have their mouths filled with laughter and tongues with shouts of joy; and I don't. I'm not joyful,

therefore I must not be a Christian." Joy is not a requ
ment of Christian discipleship, it is a consequence. It is not
what we have to acquire in order to experience life in
Christ; it is what comes to us when we are walking in the
way of faith and obedience.[3]

REMEMBER, ENDURING IS PRIMARY

How often in my own pain I felt I was useless to God, a
washout, a complete failure because I was not teaching others,
exhibiting joy, and leading the lost to Christ. But I was forgetting
what he longs to make of me: a saint who stands firm. Like James
says, "The testing of your faith develops perseverance. Perseverance must finish its work so that you may be mature and complete, not lacking anything."

Paul placed such high priority on enduring and "hanging in
there" that he wrote, "We also rejoice in our sufferings, because
we know that suffering produces perseverance; perseverance, character; and character, hope." What will give the sufferer hope?
Character. And where does he get character? By enduring
through trouble, pain, and affliction.

If you are caught in an endless cycle of pain that seems unending, dark, a veritable pit, take heart in the fact that you don't have
to be joyful to "count" as a Christian. Your testimony has not
been shattered. You are not a "poor excuse" for a Christian, or an
example of "unconfessed sin." If you are enduring, if you are
sticking with it despite your pain, you are achieving, as Paul says,
an overwhelming victory (Rom. 8:37, NASB).

Tim Hansel is a man who lives with moment by moment pain
at excruciating levels. He ends his book, *You Gotta Keep Dancin'*,
with these words:

> In the Book of Job it says that God will test us and try us
> until we "come forth as gold" (Job 23:10). Someone once

asked a goldsmith how long he kept the gold in the fire. His reply: "Until I can see my face in it."

In His marvelous and mysterious way, God keeps shaping us until he can see himself in our lives. The process is long, arduous, complex, and certainly not painless, but worth it. And we need not wait until the conclusion to celebrate. We can, if we choose, genuinely celebrate the process.[4]

Hansel argues repeatedly that we should not only celebrate the end result—Christlikeness—but the process: the pain of becoming Christlike!

As we endure, we move closer to Paul's outlook. This "momentary light affliction" is indeed producing a "weight of glory" that we will one day rejoice to witness!

There is the story of how Charles Spurgeon, depressed, feeling unable to preach, and even questioning his own call to serve God, fled in his carriage to his family home in Essex for a few days of rest. That Sunday, he visited the chapel he attended as a boy. There a lay preacher read a sermon that was actually one of Spurgeon's own printed sermons. (Spurgeon's sermons were published each week at that time throughout England, with more than 100 million copies printed in his lifetime.) As Spurgeon listened, his depression lifted; he was emotionally moved, and when the lay preacher finished, he rushed up in tears to the man to thank him effusively for his "fine words."

The layman was astonished and deeply embarrassed. He said, "Mr. Spurgeon, I don't know how to face you. I have just been preaching one of your sermons."

Spurgeon replied, "I don't care whose sermon it is; all I know is that your preaching this morning has convinced me that I am a child of God, that I am saved by grace, that all my sins are forgiven, that I am called to the ministry; and I am ready to go back to preach again."[5]

God used one of Spurgeon's own messages in a nearly miraculous way to send him back into his pulpit ready to move the masses again.

If there is an attitude that every sufferer must strive to gain, it is this: My condition is not the end. I am headed for heaven. One day this will all be millions of years in the past, a bare memory. "The suffering of this present time is not to be compared with the glory that is to be revealed to us."

That is a difficult attitude to maintain while pain is shooting through your hips and your brain is on fire. But it is a rung to grasp and cling to as we climb out of the pit of darkness back to the light. As we fight on, as we endure, we are not useless, worthless people God could better do without. No, we are one of his persevering children, heavy with Christian character, gaining an overwhelming victory.

Endnotes

1. Thomas Merton, *The Wisdom of the Desert* (New York: New Directions Publishing Co., 1960), 3.

2. Viktor Frankl, *Man's Search for Meaning,* 124–125

3. Eugene H. Peterson, *A Long Obedience in the Same Direction* (Downers Grove, Ill.: InterVarsity Press, 1980), 92.

4. Tim Hansel, *You Gotta Keep Dancin'* (Elgin, Ill.: David C. Cook, 1985), 142–43.

5. D. Martyn Lloyd-Jones, *Preaching and Preachers* (Grand Rapids, Mich.: Zondervan, 1971), 294–295.

PART THREE

Hope in the Hell, and Words for the Way

Suffering and the New Testament

We live in an age unprecedented in world history, at least in the United States. We have eliminated most of the scourges and plagues that have long haunted the world from continent to continent. While newer scourges have taken their place, ours remains a world remarkably free of pain. Many of life's most painful episodes and passages can be mitigated or even escaped entirely through miracle drugs, vaccines, therapies, and surgical techniques. Everything from headaches and backaches to depression and cancer can be controlled or eliminated with medicine's multitude of miracle cures. We are used to living productive, happy lives free of pain. When pain does invade our freewheeling lives, we douse it in any number of medications available.

Not until the 1900s, and really only since 1950, has this kind of life been a reality. And today, much of the world has few of these medical fixes. But in America, pain is something we strive to eliminate, and most of the time we can indeed avoid it.

This is also true of many of the other problems people have

faced for generations. If you are financially strapped today, there are many ways out, and even bankruptcy can be a means to start over. Debtor's prison is outdated and forgotten.

In terms of human relations, despite rising crime in the cities, most Americans live violence-free lives. The closest we come to real crime is on our highways. The worst cases still make headlines, and they remain rare.

The words that we find over and over in the Bible as synonyms for "pain," words such as *trial, tribulation, testing, affliction, persecution, suffering, anguish,* and *torment* are not common or even once-a-year experiences for many American Christians. But in the New Testament they are common, so common that sometimes one might think the Bible speaks of little else. How did New Testament authors, apostles, and teachers regard pain and suffering?

SOMETHING REMARKABLE
Just a run through several famous passages reveals some startling truth about the subject.

Starting with Jesus himself, one need only look at the Beatitudes to see a panoply of pain: the poor in spirit, those who mourn, the gentle (who do not return evil for evil), those who hunger and thirst for righteousness, the merciful (who give mercy to those who have caused them pain), the pure in heart (who have successfully struggled with their own inner pain and won), the peacemakers (who march into pain and try to untangle it), and those who are persecuted for the sake of righteousness. All are blessed. All are given high rank in the kingdom of God. And all are those who, in order to gain their respective blessings, must trek through the valley of dark days and nights.

His words stunned his listeners back then. But for us it is nearly incomprehensible. These are the blessed ones? Impossible—we must have missed something in translation! Although we don't necessarily deride the humble people, the grieving, or the meek, we certainly don't think of them as rising to the top of the heap. It is the tough-minded, the strong-willed, the ambitious, the goal-oriented, never-say-die people who really make it.

Not so in the kingdom of God.

SCRIPTURAL PICTURES OF SUFFERING

When Jesus himself was in the Garden of Gethsemane, he prayed that "if it was possible, the Father might let this cup pass from his lips." But always he added, "Thy will be done." He stood face-to-face with the greatest pain any human could suffer, and yet he could pray, "Thy will be done."

It doesn't seem so spectacular until we compare the situation to our own responses to the surgeon's knife, our tax bills, a day in court, or some form of anticipated suffering we could legitimately avoid. Jesus did not have to go to the cross. But he submitted to his Father's will. His response to suffering was not complaint or argument, but confident obedience to God's judgment.

Moving on to Acts, we see Peter and John returning from a flogging that must have left their backs, ribs, and thighs in garish, bloody welts and stripes. What is more remarkable is what follows: "The apostles left the Sanhedrin, rejoicing because they had been counted worthy of suffering disgrace for the Name."

When Stephen was stoned, his last words were, "Lord, do not hold this sin against them," perhaps recalling Jesus' own words after being nailed to the cross, "Father, forgive them, for they know not what they do."

Considering the number of media products that glorify revenge and "getting justice" for wrongs suffered, we can see that these examples of suffering stand in clear contradistinction to what our culture finds interesting and motivating. If Stephen, Peter, John, or even Jesus had made threats and then made good on them, we might find a resonant response in our own souls. But their almost passive acceptance of pain as the obvious will of God is astonishing.

THE WORDS OF PAUL

Paul, of course, remains not only a great example of pain and suffering, but also a potent expositor of the godly way to look at it. One of his greatest admonitions is found in Romans 5:3-5:

> Not only so, but we also rejoice in our sufferings, because we know that suffering produces perseverance; perseverance, character; and character, hope. And hope does not disappoint us, because God has poured out his love into our hearts by the Holy Spirit, whom he has given us.

The text functions as a remarkable progression: Suffering produces perseverance, which develops character. In turn, character leads to hope. How does this work? When one suffers, he either endures—perseveres—or he becomes bitter and angry, rejecting God and his purposes. If he endures, he learns many things: patience, long-suffering, how to be kind when he wishes to lash out, how to be gentle even though he wants to spit curses.

Suffering produces innumerable qualities in the believer that he could never have or experience in an easier life. Those qualities become character. Then as he grows in character, what happens? He studies, he matures, he learns new truths. He asks questions and finds answers. He discovers trust and obedience. He leans on his Lord. He develops in faithfulness. Above all, he feels real and genuine hope. He sees that God truly is working in his life, and therefore everything else he knows about God must be true. Finally, he sees that this hope is not fanciful or foolish or built in the clouds. Why? Because something else grows ever stronger inside him: the sensation of being loved and accepted, guided and discipled by Christ through the presence of the Holy Spirit. As Ernest Hemingway wrote in *A Farewell to Arms,* "The world breaks everyone, and afterward many are strong in the broken places."

All this from suffering. It is no small wonder Paul could rejoice in it.

THE UPWARD LOOK

But there is more. In Romans 8:18, Paul again reveals his outlook: "I consider that our present sufferings are not worth comparing with the glory that will be revealed in us." Paul was beaten with rods, stoned, flogged, shipwrecked. Surely there are few individuals who faced as much daily suffering as he. Somehow, though, he kept before his mind's eye a simple fact: This world is not the end. Whatever he had accomplished or accumulated, however much of planet earth he traversed or could call his own, he saw that it was nothing compared to what God had prepared for him in eternity.

A missionary wrote in *Guideposts* of a time when she and her husband lost their six-month-old baby. An old Punjabi woman came to comfort her, saying, "A tragedy like this is similar to being plunged into boiling water. If you are an egg, your affliction will make you hard boiled and unresponsive. If you are a potato, you will emerge soft and pliable, resilient and adaptable." The missionary concluded, "It may sound funny to God, but there have been many times when I have prayed, 'O Lord, make me a potato.'"

This echoes the attitude Paul and the others exemplified. It is something only the Spirit of God can produce in us, but with it comes fruit and qualities that change bitterness to blessedness, anger to acceptance, and coldness to kindness.

Richard Halverson, chaplain to the Senate, writes in *God's Way Out of Futility:*

It is a matter of history that much of the great art, poetry and literature, the great music and drama have come out of suffering. The man of character is usually the man who has suffered. . . . Suffering and tragedy introduce into life a dimension which nothing else can. The righteous do suffer; the most righteous man who ever lived, the perfect man, suffered more than any other; but in the words of the author of Hebrews, "He became perfect through the things which he suffered." [1]

The New Testament does not find suffering an enigma but a means to the end of joyful obedience.

A Few More

Paul writes in 2 Corinthians 12 about how God sent him a "messenger of Satan" to prevent him from "becoming conceited." Paul asked God three times to take it away. But in the end, God said, "My grace is sufficient for you, for my power is made perfect in weakness."

What was Paul's response? Not disagreement. Not a rejection. But a full-front embrace. "Therefore I will boast all the more gladly about my weaknesses, so that Christ's power may rest on me. That is why, for Christ's sake, I delight in weaknesses, in insults, in hardships, in persecutions, in difficulties. For when I am weak, then I am strong."

To the modern mind, Paul is making no sense. Embrace pain? Rejoice in insults and weaknesses? Glorify God for sending difficulties?

But from a divine standpoint, he was making more sense than the wisest of the twentieth-century sages. Paul saw insurmountable problems and trials as an opportunity for God to work. Therefore, he welcomed them.

Moreover, he was not just speaking about being "challenged"

or "stretched." He welcomed problems that defied *any* human
solution. Only then would God get all the praise and thanks.

HEBREWS
Next, we find in the book of Hebrews another sobering
verse: "Although He was a son, He learned obedience through
the things which He suffered" (5:8, NASB). It recalls Paul's famous
song about Christ in Philippians 2:5-8 that says, "Your attitude
should be the same as that of Christ Jesus: who . . . became obedient to death—even death on a cross!"

Jesus learned obedience through suffering. When we face a difficulty, we are constantly tempted to take the easy route out, the
simple way, and sometimes the sinful way. Anything to get out of
the pain. The sufferer, though, often finds there is no easy way out.
Nothing he does changes the pain, and he learns he will have to
accept it and endure it. It is then he begins to cultivate the real
qualities that will enable God to employ him in the harder work
of making disciples, leading his sheep, and speaking before sover-
eigns and kings.

Christ learned the meaning of true obedience. When everything in him screamed to be let go and to take a more pleasant
path, he chose to obey and do as his Father commanded him.
Real obedience is the ability to obey even when you don't understand, even when everything in you cries for some other way out.

THE ONE WHO PERSEVERES
Beyond Hebrews we find James, whose first few words are a
remarkable prescription for facing pain: "Consider it pure joy, my
brothers, whenever you face trials of many kinds, because you
know that the testing of your faith develops perseverance. Perseverance must finish its work so that you may be mature and complete, not lacking anything."

What quality does God most respect in men? Love? Perhaps.

Faith? Hebrews 11:5 would seem to settle it. But I would suspect that the quality that gives power to all the others is perseverance. It is love that keeps on loving and faith that keeps on believing that God values. Endurance, perseverance, keeping on keeping on is the quality that guarantees all the others. James saw it as the primary quality that God wants to develop in us toward real maturity (perfection), because it is the only one that can keep us in the fight.

Eugenia Price wrote in *What Is God Like?*

> Nowhere in the Bible does God promise to make life easy for anyone. But he does promise to be with us in all things. And if we have learned and are continuing to learn what he is really like, we find our trouble spots not obnoxious things to jump over or avoid, but opportunities to face up to the unrealities within us, opportunities to try out his life in us, opportunity to enter into a still closer and more dynamic relationship with him.[2]

And Viktor Frankl wrote, "If architects want to strengthen a decrepit arch, they *increase* the load upon it, for thereby the parts are joined more firmly together."

PETER

After James we see Peter, whose two little books function as powerful sermons to those going through terrible trials. A few words from chapter 4 of 1 Peter are helpful: "Dear friends, do not be surprised at the painful trial you are suffering, as though something strange were happening to you. But rejoice that you participate in the sufferings of Christ, so that you may be overjoyed when his glory is revealed."

Peter said that going through trials should not strike us as strange because it is the very thing for which we were destined.

(See 1 Peter 2:21 where Peter said we have been "called" to suffer and walk in Christ's steps.) It will be God's means of allowing us to experience Christ's own most personal feelings and emotions as he himself suffered. The result is that when he returns, when we see him, we will be overjoyed because we will know we have truly become like him.

Even unto Death

Last of all, there is this small text from Revelation: "Do not be afraid of what you are about to suffer. I tell you, the devil will put some of you in prison to test you, and you will suffer persecution for ten days. Be faithful, even to the point of death, and I will give you the crown of life" (2:10). It is reminiscent of Christ's own words to his disciples in Matthew 10:28: "Do not be afraid of those who kill the body but cannot kill the soul." And Matthew 10:17: "Be on your guard against men; they will hand you over to the local councils and flog you in their synagogues."

God did not tell the people of Smyrna that they would escape pain and persecution. He did not even promise that they would eventually get out of it or that it would end. Rather, he assured them that by remaining faithful unto death they would receive a crown of life in heaven. That was to those Christians power enough to enable them to face the lions while singing hymns.

Some Observations

What can we conclude from these Scriptures?

First, there is no sense of a desire to instruct believers about how to escape pain. Rather, the focus is always on how to think and act while in pain or under trial.

Again, as Eugenia Price said,

> God does not wave a magic wand over the head of anyone
> either in the matter of eternal life or the healing of a human

heart. Once and for all we must forget about cut and dried static processes. Once and for all we must begin to see that the Christian life is a life lived person-to-person with Jesus Christ. Together you and God work out the problems which come to you. Christians do not automatically become cosmic pets. And Christians who attempt to turn God into a cosmic errand boy, whose only work is to protect them from human suffering, have not seen the God of Calvary.[3]

NO ARGUING

Second, there is little to no remonstration with God about "Why this? Why me? What did I do to deserve this?" Though you find this in the Psalms and Job and in much of the Old Testament, it is surprisingly absent from the New. Why? Perhaps because the Spirit of God wants us to see that plodding determinedly through it is part of the cost of living in a fallen world. Therefore, what is given is not a brief answer to why, but a guidebook telling us what to do now that it has happened.

David H. C. Read, at one time pastor of Madison Avenue Presbyterian Church in New York, said this in an interview with *Time* magazine, "I believe the Christian Gospel not because it offers the best explanation of human suffering, but because it gives us the strength we need to win through."[4]

REJOICE!

Third, there is the much repeated directive to "rejoice" and "exult" in tribulation because of what it would produce in one's life. Paul and all the other writers constantly looked at results, where it was all going. They tasted the whip and saw character forming. They suffered shipwreck and looked upon it all as a chance to persevere. They had a distinct aversion for concentrating on this world and its pleasures. They saw life here only as the opportunity to do good, advance the kingdom, and glorify God.

In other words, they had a wide lens on the horizon: They felt pain and looked up and saw an opportunity to glorify and serve Christ. They were flogged and envisioned a crown in heaven. They had no money, were weak and sick, and looked up at problems so lethal and staggering there was no hope except in God. But hope they did, and through it they conquered the spiritual world for Christ.

J. Wallace Hamilton puts it this way: "I am sure that most of us, looking back, would admit that whatever we have achieved in character we have achieved through conflict; it has come to us through powers hidden deep within us, so deep that we didn't know we had them, called into action by the challenge of opposition and frustration."[5]

LOOKING BEYOND

Finally, they saw God beyond all the trouble, not behind it. There is no debating the sovereignty of God and whether he "caused" this or "made that" happen, leading to all the doubts and recriminations that result. Rather, they were content to see anything that was good as from God, and anything bad from the world, the flesh, or the devil. No matter how much affliction the devil flung at them, they never blamed God or battled through in-depth theological arguments about how could a good God allow this evil. Rather, they came at it in an utterly practical way: Evil exists because of the Fall, but God can work around evil and even work it for good—so what is there to worry about? Just trust him to work things out and focus on standing firm!

When Joni Eareckson Tada's depression reached a make-it-or-break-it point in her quadriplegia and she wanted to die, she found no one would help her. She was so helpless, she couldn't even end her pain through suicide. It was then she began to look up and cry, "God, I can't die. Show me how to live, please." Today, she says, "He didn't do it our way. I'd rather be in this chair knowing him than on my feet without him. I know who holds the answers, and I can wait."[6]

No matter how great your pain, do not despair. By enduring, by standing firm, by "hanging in there" and being steadfast even as you long for escape, you are achieving something that in the eyes of God is of far greater value than a life of ease. What is that? Christian faith. Christian character. Christlikeness.

Endnotes

1. Richard Halverson, *God's Way Out of Futility*

2. Eugenia Price, *What Is God Like?* (Grand Rapids, Mich.: Zondervan), 126.

3. Ibid, 92.

4. "American Preaching: A Dying Art," *Time,* 31 December 1979, 65.

5. J. Wallace Hamilton, *Ride the Wild Horses* (Old Tappan, N.J.: Fleming Revell Co., 1952).

6. From the film *Joni*; quoted in *Decision,* November 1979.

God *Does* Work All Things for Good

JOURNAL ENTRY— October 1, a year later
I told Dr. Monroe I couldn't take it anymore. I'm afraid I'm going to commit suicide. He told me to check into the Richardson Psych Unit.

I did it this afternoon. Nick drove me up. The unit is locked. I went into a room and had to strip. They searched everything. They also took away my Bible.

Day four: I was really out of it the last four days. Dr. Monroe prescribed some Valium, and it knocked me right out.

I went to group therapy. Most of the people here are depressed like me. No one talks much. I can't concentrate. I feel stupid.

Day eight: Making friends here. One girl named Marla arrived the other day. At dinner, she fell on the floor, had a seizure, and wet her pants. Nurses all over the place. I just sat

there staring, not even able to figure out what the right
response might be. So tonight we talked. Marla told me that
was "her detox [detoxification] reaction" to two months of
downing Quaaludes so she could sleep constantly and never
wake up. Her husband was killed recently, and her brother
committed suicide. She just wanted to escape the pain
through the Quaaludes.

She's pretty, long brown hair. Wears lots of leather.

Day nine: There's a guy here named Bill who is a schizophre-
nic. I went into his room tonight for a visit. He was filling
out the MMPI. I asked him if he wanted to play some Spades.
He grinned—he has a real funny face and screws it up into
all sorts of contortions—and said, "I've gotta finish this test. If
I don't, they say they'll beat me with the ugly stick."

The way he said it cracked me up. I think it's the first time
since I got here that I have actually laughed. It reminds me of
who I used to be.

Day ten: Marla said to me today, "You know, I'm totally
amazed. You must have the biggest family on earth." I asked
her what she meant.

"All these visitors. You have more visitors than anyone."

It's true. The church and seminary, friends, students, and
wives come out all the time. I told Marla about church and
the seminary. She answered, "It's the first time in my life, then,
that I've seen Christians like this."

Day fourteen: I learned Dr. Monroe isn't letting me out of
here till I'm well. I'm trying to keep up with my studies so I
don't have to drop out of seminary, but this truly horrifies me.
Despite my despair, I am still committed to graduating next
spring.

Day nineteen: Russ Long has visited me twice a week since I've been in here. I asked him today why he was doing this, considering that we hardly knew one another at school. He said, "Because I care." I hardly know him, but he maintains he's "in this with me." It really amazes me all the time. So many people really do care.

Day twenty: Marla and I danced to the radio tonight. We talked about Jesus. She said for the first time in her life she thought there might be something to him.

Day twenty-one: Russ Long was here again today. Brought with him a little Mattel truck. He said he collects them, then added, "When you get really down, just imagine you and me bucking down the road together, singing and praising God. I'm with you, brother." It touched me. Somehow I feel God sent him to me.

Day twenty-two: I asked Dr. Monroe to change my medication today, to try something else I found out about. I pressed him, and he finally said we'll start tomorrow.

Day twenty-four: A miracle has happened. I feel great. Myself. I don't want to write anymore lest I lose it.

Day thirty, October 31: Halloween. I'm still okay. The new medication has really worked. I was released today. I'm caught up in my studies—almost—even my thesis project. I feel really good. It all came back to me. A year of not being me and now I'm me again. It's astonishing. Thank you, Lord. Thank you. Thank you.

I look back at that hospitalization now and realize that even then God was doing something special. Because of what would happen later, my "health" would not last. The darkness would enclose me again. But I believe now his purpose was to get me out of that hospital so I could continue my studies at the seminary. At the same time, I was finding something else out in Technicolor: Despite my desperate, broken feelings, God still does work all things for good.

For so much of my own dark night, the most important thing I felt was to get out of it. I didn't care what it took. It didn't matter to me what truth might be applied. Just give it to me, and Let's End This Pain was my motto. We in America are so used to dealing with pain by taking a pill and extinguishing it that we forget the reason the pain exists is that something is wrong and has to be corrected. As Philip Yancey has so eloquently written in his books on pain, using Dr. Paul Brand's research on leprosy, pain is an important element of life. Without it, our bodies would destroy themselves. Pain is a warning signal of something gone wrong. Doctors tell us, "Don't just treat symptoms; you have to get to the root cause." In effect, that is what God does through pain. He makes us face up to the fact that something has gone amiss and must be fixed.

And yet, so much of our response to pain is that it is something we must and should try to escape—as quickly and mercifully as possible.

ESCAPE, ESCAPE, ESCAPE!

Dr. Viktor Frankl also speaks to this desire to escape the pain as quickly as possible: "When a man finds that it is his destiny to suffer, he will have to accept his suffering as his task; his single and unique task. He will have to acknowledge the fact that even in suffering he is unique and alone in the universe. No one can relieve him of his suffering or suffer in his place. His unique personality lies in the way in which he bears his burden."[1]

While I do not agree with Frankl that the sufferer is alone, his conviction that acceptance of one's condition and the task of bearing it is a unique idea. Railing against the pain only prolongs it.

For the Desert Fathers and multitudes of Christians through history, suffering was a privilege, a means by which God did a work in their lives. Their only desire was that they learn "obedience" through it and have the same attitude as Christ Jesus who "did not regard equality with God a thing to be grasped, but emptied Himself, . . . becoming obedient to the point of death, even death on a cross" (Phil. 2:5-8, NASB).

Frankl saw the key here: Suffering is not something to "escape," (since most often you can't!) as our twentieth-century mentality says, but something to face, to march through, to become obedient in, to endure, and to accept perhaps as a gift. Like Peter said to his readers as they faced suffering few of us will ever encounter, "But if you suffer for doing good and you endure it, this is commendable before God. To this you were called, because Christ suffered for you, leaving you an example, that you should follow in his steps. . . . When they hurled their insults at him, he did not retaliate; when he suffered, he made no threats. Instead, he entrusted himself to him who judges justly" (1 Pet. 2:20-23).

Clearly, we are to imitate Christ's attitude in suffering. That is, we recognize God will one day untangle it and make it right, even if for now what we are experiencing seems unjust and unexplainable. God is doing something great in our lives even as we struggle and endure. Even when with every atom in our body we wish to give up, to die, to fall off a pinnacle into an abyss and vanish—at that moment, when we keep slogging on, we are achieving, as Paul says, "an overwhelming victory." We are showing the world we are the real thing.

ONE MAN WHO STRUGGLED AND WON
Tim Hansel, who every day of his life must grind through mind-splitting inner pain because of a mountain-climbing acci-

dent, speaks of his own transformation through his battle with pain:

> My emotions were like a Duncan yo-yo. I discovered real depression firsthand. I had no idea how to anticipate the pain or cope with it. Perhaps I was going through the stages identified by Kübler-Ross in relation to death and dying. These stages apply to any kind of loss, that of a loved one or of a part of oneself.
>
> The first stage is *denial*—not believing that it is really happening. The second stage is *bargaining,* trying to equivocate with God to make deals. The third stage is *anger,* the rage that comes from within based on frustration which cannot be satiated. The fourth stage is *depression,* a symptom of both prolonged anger turned inward and guilt. The final stage is *acceptance,* realizing that what is, is—and is going to be.[2]

Hansel came to that final stage and wrote this:

> I've survived because I've discovered a new and different kind of joy that I never knew existed—a joy that can coexist with uncertainty and doubt, pain, confusion, and ambiguity. A journal entry a couple of years ago, written in the midst of the most trying period I've ever experienced, says simply, "I gave up looking for certainty—and found truth." I realized that when I quit waiting for certainty to come, I was free to discover, or rediscover, the essence of what I was really looking for.[3]

For many, such an attitude will seem inexplicable, if not impossible. But it is something God can embed in us through the hard knocks of life. He shows us over and over in the dark night that obedience and endurance are not contingent on "feeling like it."

Just as Jesus "learned obedience from the things which He suffered" (Heb. 5:8, NASB), we learn to obey even though everything in us may want to give up.

I found during that time that I kept "hanging in there" despite the pain. I wanted to give up every day. I wanted to die. I wanted to be released from the tiredness, lack of sleep, anxiety, and depression. But none of that happened, and I had to simply trudge on despite it.

That for me was a remarkable achievement. I'd never in my life "toughed out" something so terrible or hard. When I emerged from the dark night two years later, I could look upon it as a real accomplishment. Against incredible pain and odds I had "kept the faith," just as Paul had. That was something precious to me, even as a relatively young believer.

Any Christian who endures—whether it be through a business blowout, a bad marriage, the loss of a loved one, a terrible personal failure or sin, whatever it may be—by persevering and keeping the faith has achieved something remarkable. How many others give up and descend into bitterness or discard the faith for another God or belief? How many just decide to be "indifferent," accepting a "nominal faith" as their answer? How many trudge through life never having experienced a real sense of achievement or fulfillment?

God does something marvelous in the person who remains faithful despite his pain. That person discovers the real fruit of the Spirit—loving in the midst of hate and anger, learning patience against forces that would cause anyone rank impatience, discovering the real power of gentleness when he would rather lash out, and above all, learning true faithfulness and self-control when everything in his world seems to be spinning apart. It is easy to live out those qualities when all is well. But it is in adversity that the Spirit of God really shines through the believer with a radiance others see even when the sufferer cannot.

In the end, God gives them a jewel of endurance, a crown, which they know and recognize. When the going got tough, they kept going. As the going got tougher, they struggled on. And when things were the worst, they gritted their teeth and hung in. I don't think anyone who has persevered like that would exchange that badge of courage for an easier life, especially when he knows how much God himself applauds such endurance.

God's Miraculous Encouragement

Still, there are other ways God "works all things for good" besides producing real character in the believer's life through suffering. As I asked for prayer and help during that time, it seemed that the church gathered round me in ways I'll never forget. There were letters, phone calls, invitations to dinner, gifts of money—"Just do something fun, Mark. I'm praying for you"— and a multitude of other bits and pieces of love showering down on me like ticker tape in a victory parade. Even though I did not always appreciate those gifts on reception, they encouraged me.

In the Camps

Philip Yancey provides a potent example of such divine care in his book *Where Is God When It Hurts?* A pastor named Christian Reger was imprisoned in the Dachau death camp during World War II. He lost all faith in God during that first month in prison. What he witnessed, what he experienced, seeing Jews and friends and Christians treated like cattle going to slaughter, convinced him that God could not exist. He sank into deep despair and bitterness.

That first month, though, he received a letter from his wife. The censors had cut some parts out, but much was still readable. She wrote of her love for him, how much the children missed him, and then she concluded with a Scripture reference, Acts 4:26-29. Reger looked it up in his Bible. The text was part of a

speech by Peter and John after a release from prison. Peter said,
"The kings of the earth [took] their stand" against Jesus and did
to him "what [God's] power and will had decided beforehand
should happen." It concludes, "Now, Lord, consider their threats
and enable your servants to speak your word with great boldness."

Reger was not impressed with the quote, feeling it offered little
hope in his situation. He didn't much want to "speak God's Word
with great boldness," considering the trouble he was already in
for being a minister. But that afternoon, terror-stricken while
waiting in line to face the interrogators, a fellow minister he did
not know stepped out into the light. The man didn't look at
Reger, but as he walked by, he slid something into Reger's pocket.

Afraid to move or even acknowledge the transfer, Reger didn't
look at it. He remained in line and finally stood before the men
he knew could send him to his death. The interrogation went
unexpectedly well and without brutality.

Back at his bunk, sweating with anxiety, Reger drew the "gift"
out of his pocket for the first time. It was a matchbook, very precious to those in the death camps. Opening it with some renewed
joy, he was stunned to find inside no matches, just a piece of
folded up paper. When he opened it, he found written in neat
script: "Acts 4:26-29."

Reger stared at the reference, astonished. The giver could not
have known anything of his wife's letter that day. But the "coinci-
dence" was too incredible. How could it have happened?

Instantly, he knew the answer. It had to be from God, the
Lord's way of telling him, "I'm here with you; do not fear!"

Reger's faith was rekindled. He was alive again, and from that
point on he strove to serve God at Dachau.[4]

Hasn't every Christian been touched by such coincidences?
Why wouldn't God work that way, especially when on the internal, emotional level we may feel entirely abandoned by him? Feelings are so changeable. But it makes sense that in order to

comfort, console, and encourage, God would do something external, verifiable, physical, and personal rather than simply "change" the feelings.

Even in our pain, God does not leave us alone. He sends us special messages of his love through his people and even his angels. Though we may feel he himself has vanished, the flesh and blood friends and encouragers he puts around us will not and cannot be denied their words and gifts.

COMFORT TO OTHERS IN PAIN

I have seen another "good" as a result of pain. Perhaps a story will be the best starting point. Charles Spurgeon once preached about a crippling personal encounter with depression and inner darkness in a sermon on the Cross. When Jesus cried out, "My God, my God, why hast thou forsaken me," Spurgeon related his own experience, saying it was so painful he prayed it would never happen again.

Some time later, a man came to Spurgeon whom the preacher described as "one step away from the insane asylum." His hands shook; his eyes darted about; his head seemed to bulge with internal torrents. He told Spurgeon that after hearing that sermon, though, he was sure the preacher was one man who could understand the pain he himself felt. Spurgeon comforted him, counseling him out of their mutual experience of pain.

Spurgeon didn't see him again for five years. Then one evening at the college he had founded, Spurgeon spotted the man at a lecture. Spurgeon wrote, "I saw him: it was like night and day. He was completely changed."

The great preacher learned the man had been transformed by that night of comfort so long ago. Spurgeon concluded that he would go through a hundred such experiences if it meant he could help people like that to endure and to be renewed.[5]

Paul spoke of this experience in 2 Corinthians where he tells of the "comfort with which God comforts us so that we might comfort others." Who are often the best comforters? Those who have been "there"; those who have gone through the fire before us.

As I plodded through the darkness of those terrible days, strangely enough I began meeting Christians struggling with hard, overwhelming personal problems. Many would confide to me guilt and anguish so intimate they would offer the disclaimer at the start, "I've never told anyone about this." They would tell me their story, and I would immediately find a resonating empathy. We would pray and agree to be "accountable" to one another about praying and keeping in touch. I discovered that by sharing honestly with others about my own pain, they naturally opened up to me. Often people would say, "I couldn't talk to anyone about this because they didn't seem to understand. But you do."

That is not a comment on my own ability to sympathize, but on God's transforming power in the life of the sufferer. He becomes a magnet to those experiencing pain because they feel a kinship and understanding with him or her that they might not feel with others.

Unfortunately, I have met so many Christians who have little or no empathy! They are dogmatic, pounding away on their texts and proving their points, when sometimes tears, care, love, and an ear are what really communicate.

Henri Nouwen in his book *Out of Solitude* says a similar thing: "When we honestly ask ourselves which persons in our lives mean the most to us, we often find that it is those who, instead of giving much advice, solutions, or cures, have chosen rather to share our pain and touch our wounds with a gentle and tender hand."

I experienced this in a dramatic way at a party where I met a thrice-divorced woman who began questioning me about my faith, in fact, ridiculing and deriding it. We went alone to a room

and talked. I tried to convince her of the truth of the gospel, but
she wasn't interested, claiming that she had never met a real Christian; they were all hypocrites. I tried to show her why this happened sometimes, but she wasn't convinced.

Soon she began telling me her story, which involved, in her
third marriage, a divorce because her husband was a homosexual.
As she spoke with bitterness and regret, I was stirred by her words.
Then she asked, "Do you have any idea what it's like to be
rejected by your husband because he'd rather carry on a gay relationship? Do you know what that feels like to a woman? Or anyone?"

Her pain struck me so forcibly, I found myself crying as I listened. For a moment, she was stunned, peering at me in wonder
and saying, "You're really crying."

"I'm sorry," I told her. "I just feel so bad for what happened to
you."

She stared at me another minute, and then said, "All right, you
can tell me the gospel. Now I know you're for real."

It astonishes me to realize how often I have given advice,
shared the gospel, or listened to some sad story without even feeling concerned. But the experience with the darkness opened
up a door of empathy in my soul that I don't think could have
opened otherwise. It does in the soul of anyone who in pain will
continue to seek and honor God in his or her life.

More Witnesses

Dr. Karl Menninger was once asked during a lecture on
mental health, "What would you advise a person to do if that person felt a nervous breakdown coming on?"

To the surprise of many, he did not say, "See a psychiatrist."
Rather, he answered soberly, "Lock up your house, go across the
railway tracks, find someone in need and do something to help
that person."

There is the story of a woman who wrote in her diary, "My God, what will become of me? I have no desire but to die. There is not a night that I do not lie on my bed wishing I could leave it no more. Unconsciousness is all I desire."

She was undoubtedly going through a dark night of high magnitude. But eventually she decided to get on with life. She went on to found the American Red Cross and the nursing profession. Her name was Florence Nightingale.

If there is an answer to the question, What good is there in pain? then it is the same answer Paul gives to the Corinthians: "Praise be to the God and Father of our Lord Jesus Christ, the Father of compassion and the God of all comfort, who comforts us in all our troubles, so that we can comfort those in any trouble with the comfort we ourselves have received from God" (2 Cor. 1:3-4).

Ruth Graham wrote in *Christianity Today* of how Malcolm Muggeridge, at one time England's chief skeptic and agnostic of the airwaves, though in his later years a committed Christian, was invited to speak at Canon Bewes's church. Many local atheists arrived to heckle Muggeridge as a traitor to the cause. Most of the questions revolved around the issue of Why have you let us down? But at the end, Muggeridge noticed a boy in a wheelchair struggling to speak. When the boy continued with his contortions, still unable to say what he wanted, Muggeridge said, "There is someone who wants to ask me a question. I will wait and answer it."

When the boy managed only to make more agonized motions, Muggeridge stepped forward, put his arm on the boy's shoulder and said, "Just take it easy, Son. It's all right. What is it you want to ask me? I want to hear, and I will just wait."

The boy blurted, "You say there is a God who loves us."

"Yes."

"Then—why me?"

The room became funereally silent. Even Mr. Muggeridge didn't speak. But after thinking through his answer, he said, "If you were fit, would you have come to hear me tonight?"

The boy shook his head.

After another silence, Muggeridge answered, "God has asked a hard thing of you. But remember, he asked something even harder of Jesus Christ. He died for you. Maybe this was his way of making sure you'd hear of his love and come to put your faith in him."

"Could be," the boy replied.[6]

Such words and empathy are rarely won without going through the fire. But it is through that pain that God gives us the heart to speak such words.

Endnotes

1. Viktor E. Frankl, *Man's Search for Meaning* (New York: Pocket Books, 1963), 123–24.

2. Tim Hansel, *You Gotta Keep Dancin'* (Elgin, Ill.: David C. Cook, 1985), 35.

3. Ibid., 132–133.

4. Philip Yancey, *Where Is God When It Hurts?* (Grand Rapids, Mich.: Zondervan, 1977), 95–96.

5. Paul Lee Tan, *Encyclopedia of 7700 Illustrations* (Chicago: Assurance Publishers, 1979), 1314.

6. Ruth Graham, "Why Me?" *Christianity Today,* 7 September 1982.

What's God Doing?

JOURNAL ENTRY— January 2

If God is not really sovereign, if he really can't do anything about our situation, then what good is he? On the other hand, if he's in some sense "trying to help" but stymied by our sinfulness or the devil or something else, then still what good is he? If he's really not all the things my theology profs claim he is (and cite Bible verses to prove their points)—all-powerful, all-knowing, all-present, infinite, perfectly wise, limitless love, and all that—then why believe any of it?

It is a weighty issue. Suppose God is loving and good, but really impotent to help the suffering—as some writers in recent years have suggested. Then why should we love him, revere him, trust him? He's really no better than most of the other "gods" throughout history.

On the other hand, suppose he is all-powerful and majestic, but really doesn't care that much about us personally? Suppose he felt you were useful to him several years ago, but now that you have come up against this "problem" you are not functioning as well, so it is time to give you your walking papers. Certainly we would fear him under such conditions, just as the Romans feared Caesar and the Germans feared Hitler. But how could we ever love him, or worship him? He ends up being the devil.

The only other combination is that he is loving and good and wise, and also all-powerful and sovereign. Then the question is, Why doesn't he help us when we are in pain? Or, at least, Why does it seem that he isn't helping us, especially in the dark night when it feels more like he has abandoned us? Why did C. S. Lewis feel so graphically that God bolted him out when he came knocking? Why did God seem to discard St. John of the Cross, Don Baker, Sheldon Vanauken, and others?

One answer is that feeling him or not feeling him does not change the fact that he is there, just as disbelieving in the sun because you are blind doesn't diminish its light. Truth is truth whether we recognize it or not. God exists whether we believe it or not.

A second answer, though, is far more comforting. It is the fact that God does indeed aid and strengthen and build us up every moment of the day, even though we may feel abandoned. He strengthened me through the multitude of people he put in my life. Dr. Rick Cornish's congregation rallied around him. So did Don Baker's friends. Joni Eareckson Tada has written of how her family and friends helped her endure through three years of recovery and anguish. Even Corrie ten Boom relates in *The Hiding Place* the multitude of people who bolstered her through her great time of darkness. God was there all along, only he was working behind the props instead of front and center as at other times. Even in the case of Job, we see how God limited Satan's power. Also we know what James says, that in the end "the Lord [was] full of compassion and is merciful." God was there for Job, though it seemed to Job that God had vanished. It was a feeling, a perception problem, not a reality.

In fact, to take any of the major assurances of the New Testament, we can only conclude that God will never forsake us or desert us, as Hebrews 13:5 says, and that Jesus is "with us always, even to the end of the age," as Jesus himself says in Matthew 28:20 (NASB). A few words from Proverbs 3:5-6 are helpful:

> *Trust in the LORD with all your heart,*
> *And do not lean on your own understanding.*
> *In all your ways acknowledge him,*
> *And he will make your paths straight.* (NASB)

The heart of the problem is "leaning on our own understanding." Solomon meant, "Don't rely on your own perception of the situation. It is a false impression!" We look around us and see that problems have invaded our lives. Therefore we conclude that God no longer cares, or he has been weakened, or perhaps we were wrong about him all along; he really does not exist as the God of the Bible.

But this is simply our impression of the situation. And it is a false impression. Real trust means taking God at his word and believing it even when our mind seems to communicate something else.

A mundane example is how one feels upon awaking from a nightmare. The nightmare seems real, and even in those first few minutes of anxiety upon awaking, it can appear that terrible creatures are hovering around our bed ready to strike us. But a few minutes of regular breathing and returning to full wakefulness dispels the fear. When we realize it was only a dream, we can shake it off.

In the same way, the dark night of suffering, like a nightmare, crowds us in, corners us, and threatens with all sorts of powerful impressions and ideas. Letting those thoughts control, allowing them to guide our hearts and our thinking, leads only to a deeper pit of despair. But as we break out and trust, leaning on God's words, we can say to ourselves, "I feel as if he has vanished and doesn't care; but the Word says he will never desert me and his love is everlasting. Therefore, I will trust him and not my feelings."

It is just this kind of faith that God is trying to produce in the believer through suffering. It is also the purpose of abandonment and "desolation" as defined by the mystics. Through the sense of God's abandonment we discover that his Word alone holds. We realize that in the end we have no other assurance in this world but that Word, and therefore we should trust it and not our perceptions.

GOD OPENS OUR EYES TO HIS WORLD, TOO

At the same time, God opens our eyes to something else: the importance of his people. They are just as important and significant in holy living as an intimate relationship with God himself.

Today I see so many independent Christians out there pulling their Christianity up by their own bootstraps. They are trying so hard to "be what God wants them to be" and "go where he wants them to go" that they have forgotten to just enjoy the view. God longs for us to function as a magnificent living organism, the body of Christ, but instead we compete with one another as to who is the best and greatest and most godly, and who will do the most for his kingdom.

Today I see that my depression helped me accept the truth that I could not go it alone. I could not forge some giant ministry as a monument to myself. I could not "seek God" just for me, me, me, secretly hoping that all my hours in prayer and Bible study guaranteed that I did indeed get a bigger piece of the Rock than

others. How selfish it all was! How arrogant! How foolish to
think that life was limited just to knowing him better than others.
In this respect, I found this journal entry recently:

JOURNAL ENTRY— October 1975
As I was walking down the street today, I ran into a rather forlorn young man named Lorenzo. He was hurting far worse
than I was—his wife cheating on him, seventeen years old,
alone in Dallas, desperately lonely. I took him to Pizza Hut
for a meal. He devoured the pizza I ordered with gusto. I
shared about you, but he wasn't really interested. My ineffec-
tiveness, I guess, made me feel as if I'd failed. But I couldn't
help but notice that as I spoke with Lorenzo, I was dramatic,
excited, a different person. It reminds me again how important it is to relate to people, to love them and be loved.

Alfred Adler, the renowned psychiatrist, said,

> You can be cured in fourteen days if you follow this pre-
> scription. Try to think every day how you can please some-
> one.
>
> It is the individual who is not interested in his fellow man
> who has the greatest difficulties in life and provides the
> greatest injury to others. It is from among such individuals
> that all human failures spring. All that we demand of a
> human being, and the highest praise we can give him, is that
> he should be a good fellow worker, a friend to all other
> men, and a true partner in love and marriage.[1]

Rabbi Harold Kushner tells the story, in his book *When Bad
Things Happen to Good People,* of a Chinese woman whose son
had died. The woman journeyed to a wise man who told her,
"Fetch me a mustard seed from a home that has never known sor-

row. We will use it to drive the sorrow out of your life." Thinking this would be simple, she knocked first at the door of a great mansion. She told the one who answered, "I am looking for a home that has never known sorrow. Is this such a place? It is very important to me." The people immediately told her, "You've certainly come to the wrong place," and they described all the tragedies that had struck their lives in recent days. The woman commented to herself, "Who is better able to help these poor unfortunate people than I, who have had misfortune of my own?"

She comforted that family and then moved on in her search. Everywhere she journeyed, though, whether it was a palace or a hovel, she discovered tale after tale of pain, sorrow, and misfortune. Ultimately, through giving comfort, the grief was driven from her heart. She found the magical mustard seed through giving and showing compassion.[2]

MORE WITNESSES

A number of people I interviewed mentioned how giving, sharing, helping, encouraging—even when they didn't "feel" like it—had a healing effect on them. They were taken out of their despair and reminded that there had been a life worth living and that it was still there if they would just be patient and "trust and obey" despite the pain.

One friend counseled me to "share my burden" with the church. The next Sunday I stood up and commented during our sharing service that I was "so depressed I did not know whether God existed anymore" and that "I had considered suicide as the only real answer to my problems."

After that "confession," I received a note from a woman present whom I did not know personally. She referred to a number of passages in the Psalms, then said, "I have found Psalm 56:1-6 of almost 'magical' help in my depression—it lifts it off me."

That text reads,

Be merciful to me, O God, for men hotly pursue me; all day long they press their attack. My slanderers pursue me all day long; many are attacking me in their pride. When I am afraid, I will trust in you. In God, whose word I praise, in God I trust; I will not be afraid. What can mortal man do to me? All day long they twist my words; they are always plotting to harm me. They conspire, they lurk, they watch my steps, eager to take my life.

She then wrote,

I have no doubts as to the fact that our adversary wants to destroy us—our potential. Do you realize how precious you are to the Lord if Satan so badly wants you and your life? You must be set apart to do a great thing in this life for Him if your life is as badly endangered as it is. . . . Keep reading, memorizing, stay your mind on the psalmist's words. . . . I am praying for you earnestly, Mark, that you be delivered from the blackness and enveloped in light and peace.

I saved that letter, went through the Scriptures, and even referred to her words over the next weeks and months. Though her words did not suddenly zoom me out of my dark night, they made the journey more bearable. Knowing she and others were praying was a vast comfort. There is great power in the body of Christ—their love, their prayers, their words, their affirmations.

THE SOURCE OF STRENGTH

As Christians minister to us in our suffering, we see a source of real strength in one another. I found in the darkness that I was like a blind man being told about such colors as green and blue. But since I could not "sense" those colors, I had to choose to trust those telling me that it was true. In that respect, I continued to believe in Christ simply because God's people did. I didn't have a mustard seed of "feeling faith" inside of me. But their conviction kept me going.

Isn't this how the passage of faith to faith works? Could that be what Paul meant when he wrote that in the gospel "the righteousness of God is revealed from faith to faith?" Don't we initially believe because of what others have told us? That is exactly what the Bible is—a collection of the beliefs of others that has been passed down to ignite belief in us.

I'm not saying faith is not a supernatural work, or that the Holy Spirit does not work in us to produce that faith. However, the way he works is sometimes through people. Most of us came to faith because of the faith of someone else.

A PERSONAL LETTER

During those days I received a letter from Dona Aronowitz, the wife of a fellow student in seminary with whom I taught Sunday school to middle school kids. She wrote me,

> During a period of several months while Steve and I were in college, Steve went through some very deep depressions and was totally unable to cope with his daily activities and responsibilities. I saw him go from a very close walk with God, to being unable to pray, to doubting his faith completely. He went through many counseling sessions with our pastor, and as the problems grew greater, he was referred to a psychiatrist in the student health center. Nothing seemed to help. It was like a nightmare for me as well—I thought I would never be able to rest easy again. I constantly worried Steve would harm himself. . . . Though people cared, it seemed that few of our friends really understood and could identify. As the depression continued, and God did not answer our prayers for relief, our friends got farther and farther away.

It was during that time that 2 Corinthians 1:3-5 became very real to me. God seemed to be saying that he had a purpose—there was some very significant reason for Steve's continued sufferings, and there was a reason for my being involved as well. I felt that someday, both Steve and I could minister to others who were going through the same situation.

Mark, God does not allow such suffering without intending to use you in a very special and unique way. In our lives, this experience burned in the truth that God loves those he severely disciplines, and disciplines because he loves.

Dona included two quotes from other friends in her letter, and said in closing,

Several people grew in the Lord as a result of Steve's problems—mainly myself and Steve's parents. Perhaps God is using you to mature others as well. . . . Amazing to me, God did answer our prayers and restored Steve and healed our relationship in an unusual way. I don't know what the cause of your depression is, or if you will ever find the reason for it. Everyone's situation is different. But we felt that we should share these things with you and pray that you will find comfort and encouragement in them.

I did. Her faith strengthened me. Dona was the first person to reveal to me there were others who had struggled through the desert of the dark night. Though my heart still reeled with the blows of the inner anguish, I realized that this again was God's way of showing me love even as I doubted his very existence.

EVER STRONGER FAITH

How does faith grow and become stronger? Through the faith of others. Jude told us to "be merciful to those who doubt"

(Jude 22). The writer to the Hebrews tells us to "encourage one another" (Heb. 10:25). And Paul sent Timothy to the Thessalonians to "encourage them in [their] faith, so that no one would be unsettled by [Paul's] trials" (1 Thess. 3:2-3). What is such encouragement if not rekindling weaker faith with stronger?

It was in this respect that other Christians encouraged me. I would ask Bob Osburn, with whom I spent many hours discussing my depression and doubts, "Is he really there for me anymore?" Bob would inevitably reply, "I know he is, Mark. I know it!"

Such faith kept me alive in ways Bob didn't even know.

In this respect, I found this entry in my journal:

JOURNAL ENTRY— May 1

I saw *The Hiding Place* last night. Seeing what Corrie ten Boom went through in a Nazi concentration camp brought me to tears. I felt so wretched about my own incessant complaining. Who am I to scream at God about what "he's" doing to me when you see what she/they went through? Seeing it, I felt encouraged. Corrie said at the end of the movie, "There is no pit so deep that God's love is not deeper still." Somehow seeing others proclaim that is heartening. It is so important that we remind one another that God is there, that he's working, that no matter how bad it looks, his day is coming.

My pit was deep, but I knew it was far less worse than Corrie ten Boom's. Her faith and conviction stirred me and lifted the darkness, giving me a glimpse of light that reminded me God was there, even if I didn't feel him the way I once had.

Martin Luther found solace in others' faith, too. He frequently "argued with the devil" late into the night concerning the assurance of his own salvation. On one occasion it is said that he threw a filled inkwell at what he perceived to be a diabolical presence. He counseled those in such darkness to avoid being alone. In one of his "table talks," he said to a gathering, even as his own heart must have kicked at the doubt, "Talk among yourselves, so that I know I am surrounded by people."[3]

Another time he wrote, "All heaviness of mind and melancholy come of the devil, especially these thoughts, that God is not gracious unto him, that God will have no mercy upon him."

Strangely, those words held me. For that was part of what I felt inside—that God hated me, had discarded me, or had deserted me. Realizing Luther also felt what I was experiencing was potent comfort. The faith of a man who lived four centuries before transmitted to me a token of faith I could hold in my own heart.

Those suffering intense pain will be tempted to retreat from the world, from friendship, from conversation, from relationships. But that is the very thing they must not allow themselves to do. It is through his people that God will minister to us his love and compassion.

More Light

R. W. Dale (1829–1895), pastor of the august Carr's Lane Congregational Church in Birmingham, England, also was subject to the profoundest depressions. He called them a "strange, morbid gloominess." He wrote, "I do not envy those who walk through life with no questionings, no mental struggles." He struggled especially with the Christian teaching of hell and eternal damnation. It brought upon him the darkest pangs.

During one of those attacks, Dale was walking along a city street. An exceptionally poor-looking woman came up to him and said, "God bless you, Dr. Dale!" He immediately wanted to know her name.

She answered, "Never mind my name, but if you could only

know how you have made me feel hundreds of times, and what a happy home you have given me—God bless you!"

Moments later, Dale said, "The mist broke, the sunlight came, I breathed the free air of the mountains of God."[4]

Dispelling the darkness is rarely that simple. But friends, kind words, and being surrounded by those who love us is obviously a part of God's way of nursing us through the dark night. A cold, numbing question can suddenly appear supercilious against the warmth of an enfolding embrace or a heartfelt, loving word.

There is this entry in my journal:

JOURNAL ENTRY— May 4

I've been reading some interesting things about Christ in Gethsemane, how he sweat drops of blood. And on the cross, when he cried, "My God, My God, why hast Thou forsaken me?" In Hebrews where it says several times that he "was tempted in that which he has suffered," and therefore "is able to come to the aid of those who are tempted." I'm trying to convince myself that he knows what it's like to feel what I'm feeling. I'm not ready to say it, but I think it might be so. Especially that cry on the cross.

One of the major turning points for Joni Eareckson Tada during her own battle with faith after her accident occurred when a friend pointed out to her that Christ knew what it was like to be paralyzed. Philip Yancey writes:

One night especially, Joni became convinced that God did understand. Pain was streaking through her back in a way that is a unique torment to those paralyzed. Healthy persons can scratch an itch, squeeze an aching muscle, or flex a cramped foot. The paralyzed must lie still, defenseless, and feel the pain.

Cindy, one of Joni's closest friends, was beside her bed, searching desperately for some way to encourage her. Finally, she clumsily blurted out, "Joni, Jesus knows how you feel—you aren't the only one—why, he was paralyzed too."

Joni glared at her. "What? What are you talking about?"

Cindy continued, "It's true. Remember: he was nailed on a cross. His back was raw from beatings, and he must have yearned for a way to move to change positions, or redistribute his weight. But he couldn't. He was paralyzed by the nails."

The thought intrigued Joni. It had never occurred to her before that God had felt the exact piercing sensations that racked her body. The idea was profoundly comforting.[5]

A similar experience galvanized Corrie ten Boom and her sister, Betsie. Every Friday in the Ravensbruck camp there was a medical inspection. Prisoners had to strip down to nothing. They stood in long lines in the barracks as grinning guards walked by them. Corrie writes:

> It was one of those mornings while we were waiting, shivering in the corridor, that yet another page in the Bible leapt into life for me.
>
> "He hung naked on the cross."
>
> I had not known—I had not thought. . . . The paintings, the carved crucifixes showed at the least a scrap of cloth. But this, I suddenly knew, was the respect and reverence of the artist. But oh—at the time itself, on that other Friday morning—there had been no reverence. No more than I saw in the faces around us now.
>
> I leaned toward Betsie, ahead of me in line. Her shoulder blades stood out sharp and thin beneath her blue-mottled skin.

"Betsie, they took *his* clothes too."

Ahead of me I heard a little gasp. "Oh, Corrie. And I never thanked him. . . ."[6]

It is a brand of comfort that has divine power. Jesus was there. He understands. He knows what it is like. Therefore, he knows how to help. It is the truth of Hebrews 2:18: "Because he himself suffered when he was tempted, he is able to help those who are being tempted."

Knowing others have gone the same way as us is powerful comfort. Even to the point of seeking out such people who have experienced deep pain, the saint in the dark night must not shrink from sharing his or her story and finding a kindred spirit. It is through such people that Christ reignites the "flickering wick" and the smoldering wax. The secret of Christ's power while he was on earth was that he walked among a suffering people and he cared. He healed them. He knelt by their beds of affliction. He took their hands and raised them to their feet.

To those who suffer, he does the same through his people.

Endnotes

1. Viktor E. Frankl, *Man's Search for Meaning* (New York: Pocket Books, 1963), 104–106.

2. Harold Kushner, *When Bad Things Happen to Good People* (New York: Avon, 1983).

3. Walter Trobisch, *Love Yourself* (Downers Grove, Ill.: InterVarsity Press, 1976), 47.

4. Warren Wiersbe, *Walking with the Giants* (Grand Rapids, Mich.: Baker Book House, 1976), 45.

5. Philip Yancey, *Where Is God When It Hurts?* (Grand Rapids, Mich.: Zondervan, 1977), 118–119.

6. Corrie ten Boom with John and Elizabeth Sherrill, *The Hiding Place* (Old Tappan, N.J.: Spire Books, 1971), 195–196.

THIRTEEN

God's Sovereignty

How does the dark night relate to God's sovereignty? Is he really in control of "all things" in the universe? Can anything happen outside his plan? Is personal suffering somehow ordered and orchestrated by God?

Reducing life in our world to some idea of a divine blueprint boggles my mind. Just figuring out how God could possibly have planned out someone's day in some cosmic sense, let alone the days of everyone who has ever lived, seems improbable if not downright impossible. Why would he go to that much trouble? What of natural law, cause and effect, action and reaction, and so on? Is it really necessary for us to speak of a "God who is in control" of everything that happens in this world? And if he is, what of evil? If he really is in complete control, then, isn't he responsible for it, if not blamable?

And what of the individual who lies on a bed, his mind gouged by shooting pains through his chest and heart? Or the unfortunate child who contracts AIDS because of a transfusion of tainted blood? Or the family whose minivan is crunched between two semis, their bodies burned beyond recognition, as happened in my hometown this week? If God is sovereign, really "in charge," how does his sovereignty relate to these incidents? If such people lapse into bitterness or anger at this God who "runs" everything, isn't it understandable? How could any of us justify God's action, or inaction, as the case might be?

THE ISSUE

The issue of God's sovereignty is probably the most difficult of all theological problems. In theory it is profoundly comforting. But when we get down to specifics, to people in intense pain, the questions can become mystifying and mind-boggling. In many ways, the truth of God's sovereignty is as mysterious as it is biblical.

To start from the beginning, we see in the Garden of Eden that God gave Adam a single command: "Don't eat the fruit of the tree of the knowledge of good and evil, or you will surely die." Adam and Eve both ate and plunged us into this disaster called earth. Omniscience means that God knew Satan was loose in the universe. He also must have known all the ramifications and possible results of allowing Satan to tempt Eve and then Adam.

However, such insights are *our* deduction. Nowhere in Scripture does God intrude on the episode. It all happens while he is absent.

It is an interesting thought—because if we believe in the omniscient, omnipotent God of the Bible, we want to answer the question: Could God at any time have stopped the process? Presumably. But he didn't. Why? No one knows.

The Spirit provides no historical data concerning God's thoughts, actions, or desires. All we have is his command and man's failure.

That leads us to an interesting question: What is the use in raising the issue at all? We can't answer it unless God tells us the answer. So why speculate? It only leads to huge theological battles that often lead to broken Christians and bleeding denominations all over the landscape.

The fact is God is not concerned to tell us what he thought. He only shows us what he said, what Adam and Eve did, and how he ultimately responded.

MORE DISASTERS

Moving on through history there is Cain and Abel, the Flood (which is completely God-caused), and the Tower of Babel. Soon we find God's command to Abraham to sacrifice his son, Isaac. There isn't any data in Scripture about Abraham's feelings on this remarkable command beyond what it says in Hebrews 11, that Abraham "considered that God is able to raise . . . the dead" (NASB), and so could go ahead with the sacrifice on that belief. But I wonder if Abraham didn't suffer some anxiety and even doubt. Surely he didn't approach it with the blasé offhandedness in which the Scripture so baldly presents it. In fact, if he had, it could not really have been the test it was. God had to ask for something so significant that Abraham's true loyalties would be shown. Thus, it is almost certain that Abraham felt real anguish about the command.

To look at this from one standpoint, the whole situation looks like a colossal case of divine sadism.

Yet we regard it as a tremendous proof of faith in the history of God's people. Preachers cite it as a sublime example of commitment and love on the part of Abraham toward his God. And yet, what God was asking Abraham to do was human sacrifice, an evil practiced only by the worst pagans. We are forced to ask, How can God require this of someone? Was it that necessary?

There can be no answer there but yes, unless we are to assign to God a level of caprice and malice equal only to a monster like the Nazi doctor Mengele.

Thus, we ask again, Why was it so necessary? From the text we know only one reason: God wanted to find out how committed Abraham was to him. But if God is omniscient, didn't he already know?

We can do some topsy-turvy theological reasoning about the difference between God knowing in eternity and God working it out in time. Nonetheless, the Holy Spirit never offers any divine commentary on this event except to give us the bare details of what happened. Why? Perhaps to spare us an encyclopedic barnstorming through the mind of the eternal God, which would be impossible for us to grasp anyway.

JOB, PERHAPS THE GREATEST EXAMPLE

Job poses the greatest contradiction. Satan appears before God's throne. God asks him if he has noticed his faithful servant Job. Satan has, but remarks that if God only took down his protective hedge and destroyed everything Job cared about, Job would curse him to his face.

So what happened? God put Job into Satan's hands. And Satan did his worst.

As the story goes on, Satan fails to manipulate Job into cursing God. When he returns to God's throne, the same exchange takes place and God seems almost repentant, saying, "Job still maintains his integrity, though you incited me against him to ruin him without any reason." God is accepting responsibility here, even if it was Satan's hand that did the ruining.

So Satan again does his worst, and Job remains a stalwart believer, even though for the next thirty chapters he rails at God without intermission. And understandably so! Job was a true believer in God's sovereignty. Repeatedly, he challenges God to show him his sin. He wants to know why God has "allowed" this to happen. Over and over, he asks God to come down and just lay it out before him. He's open. He's willing. He'll listen.

When God finally does speak, he appears as an imperious lecturer who shows ad infinitum that he is far wiser than Job. In effect, God says, "Who are you to challenge my wisdom when you don't even know how the foundation of the world was laid?" In the end, Job repents in sackcloth and ashes, and God doubles Job's estate and restores his health and gives him seven more children (his first seven children awaited him in heaven).

The book of Job contains many powerful and glowing insights into the horror of human suffering. But one question the book—and the Bible as a whole—never directly answers is the one we are looking at: Why does God allow suffering? To prove Satan wrong about why people love God? Perhaps. To show the world that Job (and other believers in the same situation) are the real thing? Certainly. To lay waste the argument that all suffering is a result of sin? Absolutely.

But why such overkill? Isn't there a better way?

Certainly we must answer no, there was no other way, if we are to continue to think of God as wise, good, loving, and holy.

But then the Holy Spirit throws one more wrench into the works: It is never stated in the book that Job himself ever learned why he suffered. He knew nothing of Satan's taunts and God's answers. (If he had, it might have promoted even greater paroxysms of theological pain for him.)

Why does the Holy Spirit throw us these incredible biblical hardballs?

On top of it all is us. We do know why Job suffered. We have the story. How many of us might wonder if even now Satan is lobbying heaven for a chance to do us in and provoke us to reject and curse God?

So how does all this fit into the landscape of God's sovereignty? How can God in one breath proclaim his righteousness and holiness, and in another allow an innocent man to be put through mortal hell to prove a point?

THE CLEAREST CASE OF ALL

Job is probably the worst case of human suffering. But Jesus remains the most puzzling and yet clearly delineated example in biblical history. His death on the cross was prophesied repeatedly in the Old Testament. He warned his disciples over and over that this was where he was headed. And after he died and rose, the writings give us even more indisputable statements of God's planning and will. First, Peter says in Acts 2:23, "This man was handed over to you by God's set purpose and foreknowledge." In chapter 4, Peter says that Herod, Pontius Pilate, the Gentiles, and the people "did what your [God's] power and will had decided beforehand should happen" (Acts 4:28).

There's really no way around it: God planned and willed that Jesus would suffer from before the beginning of time. The theology of that pain is made clear in Scripture: Jesus was bearing the penalty of sin so that we might be redeemed.

Us

So can we conclude that such suffering will be the same for us? Does God will and plan it just as he did with Jesus? There are Scriptures that seem to indicate that is so.

- Acts 14:22: "We must go through many hardships to enter the kingdom of God."
- Romans 8:36: "For your sake we face death all day long; we are considered as sheep to be slaughtered."
- 2 Corinthians 4:11: "We who are alive are always being given over to death for Jesus' sake, so that his life may be revealed in our mortal body."
- 2 Corinthians 12:7-8: "To keep me from becoming conceited

because of these surpassingly great revelations, there was given me a thorn in my flesh, a messenger of Satan, to torment me. Three times I pleaded with the Lord to take it away from me."

- Ephesians 1:11: "In him we were also chosen, having been predestined according to the plan of him who works out everything in conformity with the purpose of his will."
- Philippians 1:29: "For it has been granted to you on behalf of Christ not only to believe on him, but also to suffer for him."
- 1 Thessalonians 3:3: "You know . . . that we were destined for them [tribulations, persecution, and afflictions]."
- 1 Peter 3:17: "It is better, if it is God's will, to suffer for doing good than for doing evil."
- 1 Peter 4:19: "So then, those who suffer according to God's will should commit themselves to their faithful Creator and continue to do good."

These are only a few select Scriptures that indicate God is intimately involved in our lives, both in our suffering and in bringing on suffering.

ON THE OTHER HAND . . .

Yet at the same time, there is also a distinct sense in which Scripture shows that suffering has other causes as well. Consider these verses:

- Acts 2:23: "You, with the help of wicked men, put him [Christ] to death by nailing him to the cross."
- Acts 5:30: "The God of our fathers raised Jesus from the dead— whom you had killed by hanging him on a tree."
- Acts 21:30-31: "The whole city was aroused, and the people came running from all directions. Seizing Paul, they dragged him from the temple. . . . While they were trying to kill him, news reached the commander of the Roman troops."

- Romans 1:13: "I do not want you to be unaware, brothers, that I planned many times to come to you (but have been prevented from doing so until now)."
- 2 Corinthians 11:23–26: "I have worked much harder, been in prison more frequently, been flogged more severely, and been exposed to death again and again. Five times I received from the Jews the forty lashes minus one. Three times I was beaten with rods, once I was stoned, three times I was shipwrecked, I spent a night and a day in the open sea . . . and in danger from false brothers."
- Galatians 1:7: "Evidently some people are throwing you into confusion and are trying to pervert the gospel of Christ."
- 1 Thessalonians 2:18: "For we wanted to come to you—certainly I, Paul, did, again and again—but Satan stopped us."
- James 5:10–11: "Brothers, as an example of patience in the face of suffering, take the prophets who spoke in the name of the Lord. As you know, we consider blessed those who have persevered. You have heard of Job's perseverance and have seen what the Lord finally brought about. The Lord is full of compassion and mercy."

All these Scriptures indicate just the reverse of the above section: Evil happens and though God is there (and may even be with us through it), there is no statement that he was the cause of these things, or even that he "allowed" them for some purpose. They are just stated as having happened without any comment on God's personal thinking.

This is something very common in Scripture. One text says or implies one thing, and others can imply just the reverse. In the end, one "fact" or "truth" is challenged by another that is completely contradictory. Theologians call such problems "antinomies"—something against the law or norm.

How does one put it all together? We see two opposite but

equal truths: (1) God has a plan formulated before the foundation of the world that includes everything that happens; (2) and moral beings (people, angels, demons) make real, uncoerced choices that can lead to good or evil.

In other words, everything fits into God's preordained plan without acting as if anything was preordained or planned. God's plan is there, but it never intrudes on us as we wend our way through this world. That is, life never *appears* to happen according to plan, even though Scripture says it does. How can this be?

ANOTHER STANDPOINT

Before answering that question, take a look at it from this direction. What if God doesn't have a plan (as writers such as Harold Kushner propose)? What if he doesn't know what's happening or where it's all going? What if people, angels, and animals do what they want and God has no ability to administrate it, or at least guide it however subtly toward the conclusion he desires? What if God really can't do anything about the troubles in our world? In other words, what if he isn't sovereign? What if he is just a "watcher" and "hopes it will all turn out"? How then could we ever be sure of heaven, eternal life, forgiveness, or anything else?

Have you ever gone fishing and gotten the line tangled up? Sometimes, a bad enough tangle can reach such terrible proportions that it is better to cut the line and start over. Just throw it in the trash, go to the store, and buy another hundred feet.

If God has no plan, it would seem to me he would end up with a hopeless tangle every time. Sooner or later, he would have to cut his losses and start over, or turn to another hobby.

But God can't do that. Once he threw out his fishing line, he was stuck. So look at the tangle he has. The world today is, if anything, in more of a colossal mess than it ever was. If God doesn't have a plan, if he doesn't know how to untangle it and get it operational, he'll have little choice but to trash it all.

If he can't fix this mess we're in, why should any of us trust him, love him, worship him? If he is that incompetent, how is this merry muddle going to inspire our deepest respect and reverence for him as our Creator, Lord, and leader? We have already looked at the fact that human history is part of God's means of winning the unfallen angels back to full allegiance. How could he hope to accomplish that if he really has no idea what he is doing?

A THIRD WAY

It is obvious that both sides of the sovereignty question have their problems. But maybe there is a third way.

What if God is sovereign, but he has chosen to limit his sovereignty over the world to only those times when it is absolutely needed? That is, what if most of the details of history happen according to natural laws that God has embedded into the fabric of the universe? What if God lets us make real choices and only intercedes when he chooses to, allowing things to take their natural course by natural human interaction, reaction, and re-reaction? This eliminates the problem of God being the blamable cause for evil. And it also appears to be the way he actually does work.

We must remember there are two planes of operation here. One is God in eternity. Omniscient, sovereign, all-powerful, on this plane God's plan is all worked out to the smallest details. But none of us know what that plan is until it actually happens in time and space. Knowing that God has this plan is helpful and encouraging. But what we really need to see is how God works in time and space. How does this happen?

Three points may be helpful:

1. God has a plan, but from a human perspective it looks more like a "general plot line." How God gets from A to B includes

human choices, natural laws, and the normal process of human relations and interaction. From our perspective it may look as if God isn't present at all.

2. God allows human history to take place "as it will," according to natural and interpersonal laws. Most events, problems, and "situations" happen without any divine action.

3. God intercedes only when he deems it necessary. When he does intercede, it is very subtle, a kind of divine "tweaking" of circumstances to get them to go where he wants them to go.

In this scenario, God's sovereignty is not a cudgel, forcing everything to fit into a lofty, eternal plan. But it is a behind-the-scenes source of strength and assurance. He is always there, ready to act, ready to respond to prayer and needs, and always leading events toward his ultimate goal, which is the redemption of Creation and his people, the advance of his kingdom, and the final dissolution of evil.

You can see this kind of sovereignty operative many times in Scripture. When Moses went to Pharaoh, demanding that he free Israel, there were times when God "hardened" Pharaoh's heart to move him to make certain decisions.

When Abraham let King Abimelech have Sarah as a wife, God orchestrated circumstances to stop a disaster (see Gen. 20). He spoke to Abimelech through a dream and through circumstances.

When Jacob fled from Laban, God spoke to Laban to prevent him from doing harm to Jacob (see Gen. 31).

The whole book of Esther is a marvelous example of God's providence. Repeatedly, it shows God working behind the scenes to save his people from destruction, even though his name is never mentioned.

Over and over in Scripture we see this pattern: a situation arises, problems ensue, God's people get into trouble, and then

God "nudges" one person here and another there to bring about his desired results.

Ultimately, this means God knows precisely what is happening in his world at any moment. He has planned his activities to the smallest detail. But at the same time, his actual work in human events is so subtle and a part of the fabric that it is almost invisible. This allows for human freedom and at the same time ensures his ability to keep everything moving toward his final goals.

DID GOD CAUSE MY SUFFERING?

Beyond it all is this argument we humans have about why our particular form of suffering happened: Why me? Why this? Why doesn't God take it away? The truth is, God rarely answers that question for any of us.

It all comes down to the fact that evil happens because we are in an evil world. So why blame the obvious evil of suffering on God? Why see God as causing any evil in the world? Why not look at it the way the Bible looks at it: Evil exists and sometimes God works with it, and sometimes he works around it, and sometimes he works through it. But he always works it for good in the lives of those who love him.

The whole issue of cause and effect—Did God cause my suffering?—really doesn't matter. From a human perspective, he never causes evil to happen anywhere anytime, so there is the end of it.

What matters is that we are in it and God can help us in the midst of it and ultimately lead us out of it. That is the limit of what he has revealed. "I'm with you always." "I will be with you in the fire. When you walk through the waters, I will be there!"

God has not spoken in Scripture about his sovereignty so that we can argue hours into the night why he did or didn't let such and such happen. He has shown us this truth so that we can take comfort. "Nothing that has happened has caught me unaware," he is saying. "I knew it would happen. I have planned a way for you to go through it, and in the end you will triumph!"

Scripture rarely tells us the whys of life. Rather, it offers advice, counsel, and guidance about what to do when bad things happen. "Now that this has happened, this is what you need to do."

Eugenia Price writes, "If we will give our suffering to him freely and expectantly, without fighting him for 'causing' it, we will find that he will make some form of creative use of it. He will not waste even pain and suffering."[1]

On the edge of the Grand Canyon, friends and relatives held a memorial service for the victims of a tragic midair plane collision. One young man cried out in the middle of the pastor's message, "Where was God when this happened?" The minister replied, "God was in the same place he was when cruel men took his only Son and crucified him on a cross."[2]

To the suffering, God does not offer long, weary explanations; he gives us himself.

SOME FINAL THOUGHTS ON GOD'S SOVEREIGNTY

We should beware of turning God's sovereignty into an excuse for doing nothing or a reason to blame him for what has happened to us. I guess if I could sum up the issue in a succinct statement, I'd put it this way: If you are a person going through deep suffering, much can be relieved if you simply will cease asking questions that have no answers. If God did not spare Christ for us, will he spare anything else?

But know this, kindle this, keep it strong and pure in your heart: God is sovereign. He knows you and loves you. He will never forsake you. His pain for you is even greater than your own pain. He understands and hears your cries. He cares. And he plans to bring you through this. He will bring you safely to his heavenly kingdom where righteousness dwells.

That is what sovereignty means. That is why it is such a precious doctrine.

In *A Grief Observed,* there is C. S. Lewis's shocking but stimulating entry on his own problem with God's sovereignty in the midst of his pain:

> I tried to put some of these thoughts to C. this afternoon. He reminded me that the same thing seems to have happened to Christ: "Why has thou forsaken me?" I know. Does that make it easier to understand?
>
> Not that I am (I think) in much danger of ceasing to believe in God. The real danger is of coming to believe such dreadful things about Him. The conclusion I dread is not, "So there's no God after all," but, "So this is what God's really like. Deceive yourself no longer."[3]

He says, though, in his next entry:

> The terrible thing is that a perfectly good God is in this matter hardly less formidable than a Cosmic Sadist. The more we believe that God hurts only to heal, the less we can believe that there is any use in begging for tenderness. A cruel man might be bribed—might grow tired of his vile sport—might have a temporary fit of mercy, as alcoholics have fits of sobriety. But suppose that what you are up against is a surgeon whose intentions are wholly good. The kind and more conscientious he is, the more inexorably he will go on cutting. If he yielded to your entreaties, if he stopped before the operation was complete, all the pain up to that point would have been useless. But is it credible that such extremities of torture should be necessary for us? Well, take your choice. The tortures occur. If they are unnecessary, then there is no God or a bad one. If there is a good God,

then these tortures are necessary. For no even moderately good Being could possibly inflict or permit them if they weren't.[4]

By going to the Lord, pouring out his feelings in words on paper, Lewis emerged from his grief an even more committed Christian. He realized that sovereignty, while in some ways a terrible truth, also had great power. It meant that we truly are in the hands of a good, loving God. I for one would rather be in his hands than anyone's. Like Job said, "Though he slay me, yet will I trust him."

Don't Give Up

We question and question and question, and the answer is not hard. Trust and obey. Give and keep on giving. Share your heart. Be honest. Enjoy the good things of life. And when things are tough, remember that it wasn't always this way, and a time is coming when it will never be this way again!

If you are in a dark night, take comfort in this grand doctrine of God's sovereignty. It means God is ultimately doing something magnificent in your life, and even if you don't see it now, he will continue to bring it to pass. It promises us as we plug away, as we hang in there and keep on keeping on, that God is there, God is working, and God is leading and doing good. Sovereignty backs up the truth of "I am with you always, even to the end of the age." Sovereignty ensures that he who said, "I will perfect you" will make it happen. Sovereignty fixes in rock the truth that God indeed "will never desert us nor will ever forsake us." If God is not sovereign, every word in the Bible is suspect.

But because he is, we can rely on him as firmly as we rely on the sun to rise again tomorrow. And in fact, more so.

Endnotes

1. Eugenia Price, *What Is God Like?* (Grand Rapids, Mich.: Zondervan, 1973), 97.

2. Joyce Landorf, *Mourning Song* (Old Tappan, N.J.: Fleming H. Revell Co., 1974), 74.

3. C. S. Lewis, *A Grief Observed* (New York: Bantam Books, 1976), 5.

4. Ibid., 49–50.

FOURTEEN

"What Is God Trying to Teach Me?"

JOURNAL ENTRY— March 17

I keep going back to that day when all this happened, when I felt jealous of M—— and his fiancée. I keep trying to change it in my mind.

I ask God, "What are you trying to teach me?" I wish he'd just teach me and get it over with so I could get out of this state.

But is it that simple?

Pain and suffering lend themselves to harsh thoughts, labyrinthine analysis, wishful thinking, cold, numbing regrets, angry questions, frustrating inner prayer-storms, and a strange inner conviction that daylight will never come again.

As the fire storm in my own heart leaped higher and higher, I constantly pressed God to know what he was trying to teach me—as if he also was frustrated by my inability to get the point!

With Job, I cried, "Teach me, and I will be quiet; show me

where I have been wrong!" (Job 6:24). I thought that if I simply figured out what the lesson was, if I simply grasped that dynamic truth and got the immutable thing inscribed permanently onto my heart, I would certainly be set free from all this psychic pain.

But no matter what I did, I couldn't figure it out. God seemed to be hiding it somewhere, and I had no idea where to look. I felt as if he was standing back at times snickering, rubbing his hands gleefully, and saying, "I bet he won't find it today; I really hid it good this time." It was like a game of hide-and-seek where all the kids have given up and gone home because the backward kid is "it" this time.

Even Worse

What was worse was the fact that the kinds of questions I asked I knew deep down were unanswerable. Was God going to write it in the sky? Could I expect some prophet to "pop in" and deliver a personal message from Jesus?

The questions were harrowing. They hammered away at my soul like a chain gang. Like clockwork, I always came away ever more convinced that the secret truth I had been missing was somewhere out there, and if I would just find it, everything would go back to normal.

On reflection years later, I have to ask, could it have ever been that simple? Are trials and tests and troubles God's chalk and blackboard? And is some clause of truth, some potent platitude, all he is driving at when he allows us to go through the spiritual wringer?

Do children suffer from AIDS and die early, forlorn deaths to "teach" us something? Was World War II some cosmic lesson? Well, then, what in? Did Joni Eareckson Tada and others like her become quadriplegics simply to learn a few principles most of us might rather learn by rote rather than by tragic experience? Was my own darkness God's personal tutorial? If so, in what? What exactly was he trying to teach me?

Strange, even at the time I probably would have answered all those questions with a resounding no. "God doesn't send pain just to teach us a lesson. It is much bigger than that."

And yet, my logic couldn't convince me. I was sure there was still some secret out there. If I could only discover it, that would return me to my rightful Christian bliss.

Bertrand Russell, the English atheist and philosopher, wrote in his autobiography, "What else is there to make life tolerable; we stand on the shore of an ocean crying to the night, and in the emptiness sometimes a voice answers out of the darkness. But it is the voice of one drowning, and in a moment the silence returns and the world seems to be quite dreadful. The unhappiness of many people is very great, and I often wonder how they endure it."

Russell was echoing the despair of my own soul. I wondered if I too wouldn't end up a rank atheist while still a student at a conservative seminary!

COULD GOD EVER ANSWER?

Gradually, though, I hit upon the question that stilled my soul a bit: Could God ever give me an adequate, satisfying answer to what I was experiencing, under any conditions? I knew that was probably impossible, so it all came back to the issue of trust. Could I trust that Jesus really knew what he was doing? Could I trust that he would get me to heaven in one piece? Could I—and would I—trust that though he could not adequately explain it all to me, he himself understood it and was working through it all along?

That appeared to me to be the heart of the matter.

It was then that I had to ask some hard questions about how God does transform us. Is it primarily by memorizing a series of moral principles? Is all that is involved a recitation of the Ten Commandments? If it is, then the kind of trial I and others have experienced would seem to be a rather sadistic teaching methodology. Why not just tell us to look up "trial" in the concordance, read the appropriate references, and conclude, "Oh, now I get it. Thanks!" and then, by all means, get on our way?

Because it doesn't work that way.

A CONVERSATION WITH GOD

Sometimes I would picture myself having a personal dialogue with the Lord. I would imagine all I would say if he would come down, take a seat in the easy chair, and say to me, "All right, here I am. Ask me any question you wish."

"Well, Lord, you know I've been struggling with this depression and all. I'd really like to know what you're trying to teach me."

"'Trying?'"

I'm quick to backtrack. "Not to question your ability to teach, Lord. Not at all. But what precisely are you teaching me through this thing?"

I imagine him saying, "What makes you think I'm teaching you something?"

"You mean you're not?"

"It's not that I am, and it's not that I'm not. I just don't think of this as a means to teach you something particular and specific. Teaching you something isn't the issue."

"Well, then, what on earth are you doing?"

"Exactly what I've said in my Word—'conforming you to my image,' making you 'a disciple,' 'renewing your mind,' helping you learn to glorify me and enjoy me as a person and friend—things like that."

"All right, sure, but why all this pain? Why me?"

"Everyone goes through a different process. No one is the

same. I should think you'd have understood that. But more importantly, why shouldn't you go through it?"

"That's rather nasty of you, suggesting I deserve it."

"I'm not suggesting anything of the sort. I'm not saying you should or shouldn't go through it at all. Or that you deserve it. Very little happens in this world that way. But why do you think you should be spared pain? Do you expect a life of ease in this world?"

"Well, no."

"It's just that you didn't expect this particular kind of pain."

"Right."

"You expected a broken leg, or maybe operable cancer, or to go through a traffic accident, correct?"

"Something like that."

"Well, fortunately or unfortunately, this is the pain that happened to you. I didn't particularly choose it or not choose it; it just worked out that way."

"But what about your sovereignty, Lord?"

"What about it?"

"You are sovereign, aren't you?"

"Absolutely."

"Then you could have prevented this pain?"

"I suppose."

"You suppose!"

"Sovereignty doesn't work that way."

"What do you mean?"

"That I choose everything that is to happen and then it happens. That I lay it out on a sheet or a timeline or a blueprint, and then it all just unfolds that way."

"Well, then how does it work?"

"It's far more complicated. Remember, we're dealing on a worldwide level, with more than 5 billion people—did you ever think how many hairs that is?"

"Hairs?"

"On their heads. You know—I know the number of hairs on your head, from my speech to the disciples."

"You don't know how many?!"

"Of course I do. But suppose I told you to start counting them all and keeping perfect records."

"It's impossible."

"That's how I feel about explaining my sovereignty."

"Okay, okay, but how is this experience perfecting me?"

"Trust me, Mark, it is."

"That's what really galls me. It's always 'trust me on this' and 'trust me on that.' Why do I have to just trust you about it?"

"What else would you suggest I tell you to do?"

"Why can't you explain it to me? All I want to know is why I'm going through this. Is that so hard?"

"All right, which do you want—the genetic explanation, the psychological gambit, the body chemistry consideration, the descent from Adam element, the North American WASP orientation, the A versus B personality plot line, the . . ."

"Hold it! Hold it! How many explanations are there?"

"Remember what I just told you about the hairs on people's heads?"

"Yes."

"That's about how many explanations there are."

"Well, how do you expect me to get all that down?"

"I don't. That's why I didn't offer to give it to you in the first place."

"Well, what am I supposed to do then?"

"Why don't you just trust me?"

In my thoughts I found myself coming back repeatedly to the issue of trust. And what is trust but depending on God to help or "come through" when troubles start? What is trust in God but taking him at his word, even though we may not see precisely how it squares with reality at a given moment? What is trusting Christ but leaving in his hands matters we cannot change with the belief that he will make them turn out—perhaps years down the road—for good?

HOW WE MATURE

No one gets spiritually mature by learning a few theological facts. If God meant for all Christian learning to happen by a pastor standing at a chalkboard and giving us a detailed theological argument, then most of us would have honorary doctorates by now. If formulas, alliterated outlines, and sermonic packages were God's way, why isn't the Bible crammed with such things? The one reason that makes sense is that they are not God's means to the end of transformation.

I'm not saying such things can't help. But in God's school anything can happen, and none of it has to make human sense. In fact, he doesn't ask us to understand everything he does. He simply asks us to trust him. Christianity isn't a series of steps or facts or lessons or answers or even questions. It is a relationship with the Almighty that is as real and breathing as a wonderfully difficult and unnerving but satisfying marriage.

I'm convinced the Lord is not bent on making human sense of most of the things that happen in this world. Thinking as a human, I suspect that evil stymies him as much as it does us. Not that he isn't omniscient. But it is his very omniscience that prevents him from considering evil and sin an option. He sees demons and people making choices that lead to evil. He understands their thinking. But in the end how rational beings can make such obviously wrong choices must strike him as utterly incomprehensible. In his sight such acts are rank rebellion.

WHAT IS GOD DOING?

God is not trying to "teach us something" in any or even most of the experiences of life. He is not interested in cramming a "marriage series" or a "codependency seminar" or a "ten-step program for spiritual success" into our brains. Very little of what it means to worship and know God can be reduced to "lessons" in the classic sense.

Rather, he is building an eternal relationship. He is designing a new and perfect creation. He is crafting a nation in which every one of us will one day be flawless reflections of his own character, imagination, and spirit. He is leading us to a world that even he cannot explain to us adequately in the here and now because we couldn't understand it.

So why should we think he could explain in a few simple paragraphs why anything else happens the way it does?

FIFTEEN

If You Are in the Middle of It

What help can these pages offer a Christian who is suffering intensely?

Ultimately we all want to know, What can I do now? How can I begin to endure through this suffering with some measure of fulfillment and a sense of God's love and help?

Some of these suggestions might be helpful:

Stop trying to find answers about why. They will never come with unmistakable exactness. Many reasons are given in the Scriptures for suffering in addition to the ones I have offered. Over time you will undoubtedly latch onto one reason you see here and another there, perhaps changing your mind as you grow spiritually. But an ultimate answer is rarely proffered in this world. Rest in the fact that God loves you, understands your situation, and will bring you "safely to his heavenly kingdom." Trust that he has the answers, and perhaps one day he will reveal them. But until then, resolve to trust and obey.

Get help wherever you can. Do not think you can go it alone. As Solomon said, two ropes are stronger than one, and a cord of three strands is not easily broken. God wants us to use the resources available, whether they be doctors, counselors, friends, or relatives. I found that one of the "goods" that proceeded from my depression was a closeness and friendship with my parents that I had never had before, and especially as a zealous, preachy Christian.

Above all, stay plugged into your church home. Let the people there minister to you. If some say offensive or insulting things— "You just don't have enough faith" or "You must have done something terrible, so confess it and go on"—let your patience show and do not condemn them. God will deal with their dogmatic and ill-informed ideas in time. There is no reason for you to lash out at them or even condemn their counsel. However, if a person does become overbearing in his or her insistence that he knows why—as Job's counselors were—speak your mind forthrightly and kindly, and try to help that person understand you have heard his or her counsel and do not agree with it. Seek, if necessary, to "agree to disagree." Breaking a friendship over misguided doctrine is not worth the trouble or the pain. As Paul told the Philippians, "Let your forbearing spirit be known to all men."

Look for the good and expect to find it—in time. One of the greatest struggles beyond answering the question why is the question, What good is it doing? Open your heart to all God will show you. Let him speak. He may not reveal it immediately. But with time, he will open your eyes to things that you might have missed through the glare of your pain.

Many "goods" proceeded from my depression. Among them: a closer, more understanding fellowship with my family; close, intimate friendships with several other men in seminary; a prayer life marked by zeal and the ability to keep on praying despite setbacks; the ability to take walks as a form of recreation and a time to meditate on Scripture and pray; the reading of many new books and an acquaintance with authors I never read, from J. R. R. Tolkien, Herman Wouk, and James Michener to Benjamin Warfield, D. M. Lloyd-Jones, and John MacArthur; and a deep sense that my only hope was in Christ, his Word, and his grace.

None of these are necessarily life-transforming concepts. But for me, they were important steps in my own growth.

Practice the classical disciplines. Dr. Rick Cornish said that he came out of his dark night of depression through a rigorous commitment to practicing the classical disciplines. I asked him, "What would you say to someone who is suffering intensely, perhaps in a classic 'dark night of the soul'?" He replied,

> I'd encourage them to get into the habit of using the classical spiritual disciplines as part of their life-style—solitude, study, meditation, journaling, prayer, fasting. In the end, I guess I'd have to admit there wasn't much I or anyone else could do to immediately alleviate the pain. In a real sense, you're in it, you have to go through it, and you'll come out of it when God and you are ready. So, I'd assure them it wasn't a random happening. God is there, and he is working something in them, which, when they emerge, they will consider incredible. For me, it was the most significant experience of my life—perhaps even greater than my salvation experience. I had endured something so overwhelming that I now know I believe in God and love him because I want to with all my heart. He is worthy of that love, and I suppose I will never question it again.

Get answers to your questions. The habit of a quiet time is a start. But each of us needs that special intimacy with God that comes only through solitude, prayer, and Bible meditation. As we learn to seek him and know him through those disciplines, we gain an inner strength of light that will not dim, no matter how great the darkness.

As you have strength, go out and help others. Albert Schweitzer said, "I don't know what your destiny will be, but one thing I know: the only ones among you who will be really happy are those who will have sought and found how to serve." He was a man intimate with suffering, both his own and that of his patients. He wisely saw, though, that the way out of your own pit is by helping others out of theirs.

An elderly widow who was restricted in her activities remained eager to minister for Christ. After prayer, she realized she wasn't able to go from house to house passing out tracts, but she did have one gift: playing the piano, as she had done at her church for many years. The next day she placed an ad in her local city paper: "Pianist will play hymns by phone daily for those who are sick and despondent—the service is free." She listed her phone number, and as people called, she would immediately ask, "What hymn would you like to hear?" In a short time, she had played the great hymns of the faith for hundreds of lonely and depressed people. Often, in the course of a conversation, the respondents would share their griefs with her and she would counsel and comfort them as best she could. She testified, "That service became the most rewarding thing I ever did in my life."[1]

Keep a journal. I have shared some of the scrawlings from my journal during those hard years. Reading over the entries, old memories come back that refresh me and remind me of friends I have not seen in years, people who ministered in ways I had forgotten, and experiences that at times I wished I could forget. But most of all, I found some of my own musings about my depression and darkness fascinating. Only in looking back through it have I gained real perspective on that time. Because of it, I realize how powerfully God was working to keep me alive.

What should you write in your journal? Anything that is important to you—anecdotes, quotes, prayers, musings, biblical texts, your own struggle through an issue. Whatever is on your mind. Whatever questions trouble you. And the answers you discover. Let it flow.

Spend time alone, thinking, praying, seeking God. Henri Nouwen has written of the effects of solitude and time with God in his book about the wisdom of the Desert Fathers, *The Way of the Heart:*

> St. Anthony, the "father of monks," is the best guide in our attempt to understand the role of solitude in ministry. Born in 251, Anthony was the son of Egyptian peasants. When he was about eighteen years old he heard in church the gospel words, "Go and sell what you own and give the money to the poor . . . then come and follow me" (Matt. 19:21). Anthony realized that those words were meant for him personally.
>
> After a period of living as a poor laborer at the edge of his village, he withdrew into the desert, where for twenty years he lived in complete solitude. During these years Anthony experienced a terrible trial. The shell of his superficial securities was cracked, and the abyss of iniquity was opened to him. Then he came out of his trial victoriously— not because of his own willpower or ascetic exploits, but because of his unconditional surrender to the Lordship of Jesus Christ. When he emerged from his solitude, people recognized in him the qualities of an authentic "healthy" man, whole in body, mind, and soul. They flocked to him for healing, comfort, and direction.

In his old age, Anthony retired to an even deeper solitude to be totally absorbed in direct communion with God. He died in the year 356, when he was about 106 years old.[2]

Nouwen says,

In solitude I get rid of my scaffolding: no friends to talk with, no telephone calls to make, no meeting to attend, no music to entertain, no books to distract, just me—naked, vulnerable, weak, sinful, depraved, broken—nothing. It is this nothingness that I have to face in my solitude, a nothingness so dreadful that everything in me wants to run to my friends, my work, and my distractions so that I can forget my nothingness and make myself believe that I am worth something.

But that is not all. As soon as I decide to stay in my solitude, confusing ideas, disturbing images, wild fantasies, and weird associations jump about in my mind like monkeys in a banana tree. Anger and greed begin to show their ugly faces. I give long, hostile speeches to my enemies and dream lustful dreams in which I am wealthy, influential, and very attractive—or pout, ugly, and in need of immediate consolation. Thus I try again to run from the dark abyss of my nothingness and restore my false self in all its vainglory.

The task is to persevere in my solitude, to stay in my cell until all my seductive visitors get tired of pounding on my door and leave me alone.[3]

Read everyone and anyone to gain insight and help—especially the Psalms. The Psalms are a prayer book of people going through hard times. A multitude of the 150 psalms recorded speak to the issues of persecution, pain, God's silence, feeling enclosed by the dark, and what God might be doing in your life. Some special favorites of people I spoke with are Psalms 1, 3–5, 8, 13, 14–15,

19, 22–24, 27, 32, 38, 42, 46, 51, 63, 100, 103, 130, 142–150. Everyone has their own favorite texts. But the thing that is most startling about many of these psalms is how accurately they mirror our own feelings in the midst of pain. Consider these thoughts from one of the authors of the Psalms:

Psalm 3
O LORD, how many are my foes!
How many rise up against me!
Many are saying of me,
"God will not deliver him."
But you are a shield around me, O LORD;
you bestow glory on me and lift up my head . . .
I will not fear the tens of thousands
drawn up against me on every side.

Psalm 4
Answer me when I call to you,
O my righteous God.
Give me relief from my distress;
be merciful to me and hear my prayer.

Psalm 10
Why, O LORD, do you stand far off?
Why do you hide yourself in times of trouble?

Psalm 38
O LORD, do not rebuke me in your anger
or discipline me in your wrath. . . .
O LORD, do not forsake me;
be not far from me, O my God.
Come quickly to help me,
O Lord my Savior.

Psalm 42
As the deer pants for streams of water,
so my soul pants for you, O God. . . .
Why are you downcast, O my soul?
Why so disturbed within me?
Put your hope in God,
for I will yet praise him,
my Savior and my God.

What are these words, if not the cry of the heart that feels abandoned? Yet, as you read, you find, frequently in the same psalm, a word of faith, hope, and conviction that God will yet help and save. Rarely, only in Psalm 88, does one find abject despair. And even that psalm echoes within us a resonant chord. God does understand our fear and our despondency. He can and will do something to bring relief.

Many other books on suffering, spiritual living, trial, and how to win over various emotional problems are available. I found—as did most others—that my pain drove me to read everyone and anyone who might offer some insight into my condition. As a result, for many, going through deep pain is a time of tremendous growth in wisdom and understanding of God's ways.

Senator Sam Ervin, who presided over the Watergate hearings during President Nixon's tenure, spoke these wise words about Christian religion: "Religious faith is not a storm cellar to which men and women can flee for refuge from the storms of life. It is, instead, an inner spiritual strength that enables them to face those storms with hope and serenity. Religious faith has the miraculous power to lift ordinary human beings to greatness in seasons of stress."

Where do we find that power? In God's Word. Through reading. Through committing ourselves to finding his truth and treasuring it in our minds as assurances of God's new day.

Take walks and talk things out; reason them through with God.
Another thing I discovered through my inner psychic pain was
the power and refreshment of a good, long walk. My physical condition was much improved as I walked miles and miles every day,
just trying to find relief from the inner anguish. The walks were a
way to expend energy and rid myself of sour emotions, get fresh
air, think, think, think, clear my head, and think some more. Stuffy
rooms, my tiny apartment, and the indoor heat did little to help
my condition. But sun, air, cold, a change of scenery, and the
simple pleasure of walking is a habit I have preserved till today. A
walk does much to take one's mind off whatever tangles are inside
it. Often, after a walk, one finds the tangle is a knot far smaller
than it looked at the start.

Other people I interviewed said the same thing happened to
them:

"I really learned to pray and wait during that time just by walking and thinking."

"Prayer became a lifeline. While walking, I could pray for
hours. It had a way of calming me. Without it, I know I would
have given up."

"I spent a lot of time just thinking on Psalm 23 and Psalm 38
and many of the psalms as I walked, jogged, and simply got out-
doors. Those texts became very dear to me because I realized that
what the author was talking about was what I was experiencing."

Rejoice in the Lord. One might think that rejoicing is an impossible thing in the midst of suffering. And yet, after Job lost everything he owned, the first thing he did was rejoice: "Naked I came
from my mother's womb, and naked I will depart. The Lord gave
and the Lord has taken away; may the name of the Lord be
blessed."

After being flogged before the Sanhedrin, Peter and John
rejoiced that they had been considered worthy of suffering for

Christ's name. And Paul, when God sent him a thorn in the flesh, rejoiced in his weaknesses and problems because they made him strong in Christ.

The key is to rejoice in the *Lord*. Knowing him, being loved by him, having the assurance that he is with us and cares for us—all that is cause for rejoicing. When the disciples came back from their first evangelistic tour, having cast out demons and healed the sick themselves, they were full of excitement and rejoicing. But Jesus told them to rejoice not that they had power over demons, but that "their names were written in heaven." Rejoicing in all that God is and has and has done is real rejoicing. A person can rejoice in God regardless of his emotional state.

Brother Lawrence's book *The Practice of the Presence of God* has influenced whole generations for Christ. He was a monk who rejoiced in and praised God even though he was little more than a dishwasher. He wrote, "I know not how God will dispose of me. I am always happy. All the world suffers, and I, who deserve the severest discipline, feel joys so continual and so great I can scarce contain them."

Georgi Vins, the leader of the Baptist movement in Russia during the two decades before the dissolution of the Soviet Union, was interviewed by Reverend Michael Bourdeaux, director of Keston College, after Vins's release to the West. He wrote,

> In speaking to Georgi Vins, one cannot but be impressed by the calm and spiritual serenity the man exudes. He has no harsh words to say about those who persecuted him. He speaks of love, prayer, Christian duty, brotherly love. His trials do not seem to have embittered him in any way, but on the contrary, vest him with tolerance and undeniable authority. One feels that although he may have been deprived of physical freedom, his spirit is one which was able to soar, joyous and unconfined, in communion with his God.[4]

Warren Wiersbe, writing in his book *Be Joyful,* relates a time while he was in the hospital because of an auto accident. He received several letters from a stranger whose words always brightened Wiersbe's outlook on that day. When he was released, Warren looked the man up, and to his astonishment, he discovered a person who was blind, diabetic, and unable to walk because of a leg amputation. He lived with and cared for his elderly mother. But because of his handicaps and apparent triumph over them, he often spoke at service clubs, the YMCA, and before professional groups. He was a man filled with joy, who could rejoice because he did not look at his injuries but at his God.

It is easy to pile up examples of those who have been victorious in their struggles. But taking the steps to rejoice in God, even if you do feel isolated, fearful, and bitter, is a start. One needn't wait to "feel" joy. Rejoicing in God is simply recognizing his worth and proclaiming it within your heart regardless of feelings. Eventually, your emotions will change. They are, in fact, always changing. So obedience in this matter is not regulated or even contingent on emotions. As Paul said, "Rejoice in the Lord always, and again I will say rejoice." He wrote those words to the Philippians, people who were deeply fearful, worried about their leader, and assaulted by enemies and difficulties too numerous to think about. Yet, Paul's advice was to rejoice, for in it is great spiritual power.

Do not give up hope. To give up hope is to commit spiritual suicide. And yet, there is no reason for any Christian to give up hope even though this world looks like a dead end to him. Many people who suffer will never escape their condition. Their suffering is terminal, and they will be released only into death. What can anyone say to such people? Much. The Scriptures are full of guidance and hope to those who will struggle unto death. Jesus did. Everyone of the disciples except John were executed, and

John was banished to the Isle of Patmos. I've often wondered why each of those men suffered so. I think the answer is plain: God did not want to give them riches, happiness, pleasure, a life of ease, because that is not his way. That so many of us in America have such things is not so much a sign of God's special favor, but that he may be doing something else: showing that riches and ease do not produce the results he wants. After all, the church of Laodicea was rich and well off, and yet God threatened to spit them out of his mouth because of their lukewarmness.

Christianity is a religion of hope not because we gain everything this world has to offer, but because we have gained a place in the coming world that will go on forever. However much we might wish to preserve our wealth and gains in this place, it is a foolish pursuit. This world is little more than a giant graveyard.

Helen Grace Leschied, a writer living in British Columbia, writes in *Christian Parenting Today* of her own struggle with her husband's long-term depression:

"Where is God now?" my son cried out from the depths of his soul. "Dad doesn't belong in a place like that," he sobbed. "You always said God watches over the righteous. Why didn't He?"

I found no easy way to answer my son. My husband's deep depression and hospitalization had struck our family of seven like a lightning bolt out of a clear blue sky. We were astonished at the speed with which the condition had progressed.

The children's tall, well-built dad had always been their most enthusiastic fan. He was the family cheerleader. . . .

He taught us how to appreciate creation . . . turned Friday nights into family fun nights. . . .

But all this came to a crashing halt when my husband, at age fifty, suddenly committed himself to a psychiatric hospi-

tal, afraid of the harm he might do to himself and to his
family. . . .

The emotional devastation we felt was as real as if an
earthquake had hit and we were left standing in the rubble.

Where is God now?

My mind reeled. Through the years I'd grown to know
Him as a good Father, someone who could be trusted to do
the right thing for His children. . . .

The Lord had sustained me in other dark times, and the
lesson I'd learned at those times had proven invaluable. . . .

There have been eight lengthy confinements in various
psychiatric hospitals. Throughout the forty months there
have been only short periods during which my husband was
well enough to come home. Each time, I had allowed myself
to hope that he had come home to stay.[5]

It is a story like this that tears me. Why does God allow this
kind of suffering to go on and on and on?

I'd like to say I have an explanation for it. I wish in all my time
in the dark I could now lay out three points that were so conclu-
sive that the question would be banished from history.

But I have no immediate answer. And yet, Mrs. Leschied does.
Her article is titled, "Dancing in the Dark," and she concludes
her stark story with these words:

Wouldn't it be better if God performed a miracle of healing? I still wonder. Only God can answer that question. He
is the master composer who orchestrates our lives. Jesus himself has defined the tune he would play: "In this world you
will have trouble. But take heart! I have overcome the
world" (John 16:33).

At times the battle is so severe, all I can do is whisper,
"Lord Jesus, hold me." Then I feel his nearness, almost as

though I could touch him. And it seems to me like I'm dancing with him in the dark.

Against overwhelming odds, Mrs. Leschied continues to believe, to stand firm, to refuse to give up hope. And to dance in the dark!

I am just as convinced that God will make it right for her and her family in the end. I know this evil world is only a stomping ground, not a permanent dance floor. I know that in the end we will all truly see that "he has done all things well." I know that *he* knows why things have happened as they have.

But I do not know the answer myself. Nor does anyone else. We will simply have to trust him with that responsibility.

Remember: Your destiny is not in this world. Above all, we must keep telling ourselves, "This is not the end. This world, this place, this time is not the end. Jesus is coming again. He will hatch open a whole new world, and we will reign with him in glory."

Those words can feel like grit in the ears of someone who has climbed the mountains of joy and pleasure in this world and now must suffer. But God has warned us over and over: "In this world you shall have trouble." "This world is of the evil one." "The world will perish." We cannot cling to it, even at the height of joy and pleasure in it. We must remind ourselves, "We are made for another place, another existence. I am only here now to glorify God and serve him."

None of us who believe in Christ has to give up. We may plod. We may stumble. We may just stagger along. But God will bring us safely to his heavenly kingdom. And there we shall dance, sing, and look on his face, never again to be plunged into a world as dark as this one.

Endnotes

1. Henry G. Bosch, "Possibilities at Hand," in *Our Daily Bread,* March 26, 1981 (Grand Rapids, Mich.: Radio Bible Class).

2. Henri J. M. Nouwen, *The Way of the Heart* (New York: HarperCollins, 1981), 19–20.

3. Ibid., 27–28.

4. Myrna Grant, "What Soviet Christians Are Teaching Me," *Moody Monthly,* January 1980, 123.

5. Helen Grace Leschied, "Dancing in the Dark," *Christian Parenting Today,* May/June 1990, 67–68.

CONCLUSION
This Too Shall Pass

SIXTEEN

Out and Free

JOURNAL ENTRY— November 20
I've decided to go to Indianapolis as youth pastor to a church there. I feel I need to make some money, get my feet wet in a rough situation, and to learn to overcome my personal battles with depression.

JOURNAL ENTRY— November 24
Celebrated Thanksgiving with the Osburns and some other friends. A marvelous time eating, joking, and playing Pit. Later on, Pattie Wulff came by, and we played Scrabble. I won both times (not to brag). I think I'm becoming something of a games fanatic.

I haven't suffered too much from depression lately, not as much anyway.

JOURNAL ENTRY— January 14
I arrived in Indianapolis after a harrowing drive through the snow. I'm grateful the Lord delivered me here safe and sound.

I wrote two poems today, too. I'm actually back into writing after this long, sad hiatus. Is the depression really gone?

The first line M. Scott Peck writes in his best-selling book *The Road Less Traveled* is this: "Life is difficult."

How well we fellow strugglers know that. But there are moments of release, days of pleasure, and years when life is good. In the next days and months I would find that out anew. The depression too had passed. It just slipped away. Why?

I have no idea. All that mattered was that it was behind me. Something inside me was tingling. The "crown of life" that James had talked about for those who persevere through trial? Perhaps.

Something had happened, though. I felt new inside, free. I continued on the medication. There would be battles ahead. But I had done something I never could have predicted or expected: I had survived the worst trial of my life, and my faith, mind, and commitment remained intact. That was something I could take a special, godly pride in. The worst thing I could imagine had been hurled at me, and I had stood the test, even though I staggered and fell many times. In the end, I felt deep in my bones that I had not failed myself, my family, or God, even though it had looked that way nearly every day for the previous two years.

I ask myself today: Why did I go through that time of darkness?

I still don't know. I can think of many good things that came out of it. I can see so many wonderful lessons and characteristics that were bred into me because of it. But in some ultimate sense—why? Perhaps so this book could be written. Perhaps so I could comfort others. Perhaps so I would draw nearer to God.

And perhaps none of that. Perhaps it is something else, somewhere far ahead in eternity maybe. Why even ask the question? I won't get an answer here and now, and perhaps never.

TRUTH ON THE LINE

And how does God look at it?

I think of two favorite passages from The Chronicles of Narnia, by C. S. Lewis. The first occurs in *The Horse and His Boy.* Shasta, the hero, is sent on an adventure to save Narnia. At different points lions have appeared to speed him on his way, especially when he falters. Toward the end of the book, Shasta meets Aslan, the lion who represents Christ in the series. Shasta asks him if he thinks it was "bad luck to meet so many lions." Aslan tells him there was only one lion—him. Shasta is astonished, but Aslan says, "I was the lion who forced you to join with Aravis. I was the cat who comforted you among the houses of the dead. I was the lion who drove the jackals from you while you slept. I was the lion who gave the Horses the new strength of fear for the last mile so that you should reach King Lune in time. And I was the lion you do not remember who pushed the boat in which you lay, a child near death, so that it came to shore where a man sat, wakeful at midnight, to receive you."

Shasta says, "Then it was you who wounded Aravis?"

"It was I," Aslan answers.

"But what for?"

"Child," Aslan answers, "I am telling you your story, not hers. I tell no one any story but his own."[1]

I remember weeping as I read those words. Perhaps one day I will hear *my* story. But I am just as convinced today that that same lion—Jesus—is the one who was there when the depression first struck, there to speed me to Dr. Monroe, there encouraging me in the multitude of friends around me, there in the hospital, and there when it went all wrong again. All along, he had been there, vigilant, loving, forgiving me my anger and complaining before it ever even broke on my lips.

HE DOES FEEL OUR PAIN

A second passage in *The Magician's Nephew* is equally insightful. Digory, the hero this time, has arrived in Narnia at the beginning of its creation and accidentally brought along with him a witch who will eventually corrupt the whole new world. When he meets Aslan and learns of his power, he pleads with him to do something to help his dying mother. "But please, please—won't you—can't you give me something that will cure Mother?"

This text follows: "Up till then he had been looking at the Lion's great front feet and the huge claws on them; now, in his despair, he looked up at its face. What he saw surprised him as much as anything in his whole life. For the tawny face was bent down near his own and (wonder of wonders) great shining tears stood in the Lion's eyes. They were such big, bright tears compared with Digory's own that for a moment he felt as if the Lion must really be sorrier about his Mother than he was himself."[2]

I remember reading those words in the days of my own darkness and marveling, weeping, wondering that this was undoubtedly Jesus' response to my pain, to everyone's pain. Aslan did not try to explain it. Neither did he make it out to be less than it was. He just wept.

I think of John 11:35, the shortest English verse in the Bible: "Jesus wept."

I think of Jesus' explanation to his disciples about the blind man in John 9 when they asked, "Who sinned, this man or his parents, that he should be born blind?" Jesus answered, "It was neither that this man sinned, nor his parents; but it was in order that the works of God might be displayed in him" (NASB).

And I think of Job, who never knew why he suffered, but who, when he was confronted by the majestic God of the universe, repented and said, "I know that you can do all things; no plan of yours can be thwarted. . . . My ears had heard of you but now my eyes have seen you. Therefore I despise myself and repent in dust and ashes."

God so rarely answers why in the Bible. Why should he answer us today?

RELEASE!

Still, whatever happens to us, I believe there is great hope in the expression, God does not waste our pain. He will indeed bring out of it good, for those who will seek and love him.

Dr. Viktor Frankl, whom I have quoted so liberally in this book, would put that recognition of "good" this way:

> For every one of the liberated prisoners, the day comes when, looking back on his camp experiences, he can no longer understand how he endured it all. As the day of his liberation eventually came, when everything seemed to him like a beautiful dream, so also the day comes when all his camp experiences seem to him nothing but a nightmare.
>
> The crowning experience of all, for the homecoming man, is the wonderful feeling that, after all he has suffered, there is nothing he need fear any more—except his God.[3]

Philip Yancey, comparing Elie Wiesel's *Night* to Corrie ten Boom's *The Hiding Place,* pictured it in similar terms:

> God does not condemn our moments of despair and unbelief. He Himself set the tone by diving into earth and enduring cruel, senseless suffering. Before the final moment, His own Son asked if the cup could pass from Him, and on the cross cried out, "God, why have You forsaken Me?" The full range of anger and despair and blackness described so powerfully in *Night* is present in the Christian message—complete identification with the suffering world.
>
> But Christianity takes a further step, which has been a stumbling block to man. It is called the Resurrection, the moment of victory when the last enemy, death itself, was smashed. God, who invites Job and Corrie ten Boom and you and me to step into joy and victory, does not ask us to

accept a Pollyannaish world. He simply adds a further, mysterious layer to human experience. He asks for hope in spite
of hopeless surroundings. When suffering bleeds us, He asks
us not to reject Him, but to respond to Him as children,
trusting His wisdom and affirming as Corrie said, "However
deep the pit, God's love is deeper still."[4]

William Styron, speaking of his own exit from the incredible
psychic pain of clinical depression, offers a poignant word, too:

> For those who have dwelt in depression's dark wood, and
> known its inexplicable agony, their return from the abyss is
> not unlike the ascent of the poet, trudging upward out of
> hell's black depths and at last emerging into what he saw as
> "the shining world." There, whoever has been restored to
> health has almost always been restored to the capacity for
> serenity and joy, and this may be indemnity enough for hav-
> ing endured the despair beyond despair.[5]

Then there is Don Baker, who speaks of a period when he
floated in that interim world between illness and complete health.
A neighbor loaned Don his cabin so the now unemployed pastor
could get some time alone to fast and think and pray and seek
God's face. The dark of his dark night still was not gone entirely.

Early out, Don climbed a hill and stood by a cross where hundreds of teenagers dedicated their lives to Christ each spring, summer, and fall. He began to weep, feeling lost and confused, but
also feeling that God's call on his life had not been rescinded.
Finally he knelt by the cross and prayed:

> Oh, Father, I love You and I know You love me—even when
> my feelings tell me otherwise. I still don't understand all
> that's happening in my life or why, but I do trust You. I do

know You have a plan and even though I may never fully understand it, I still trust You.

Please, Father, let me pastor a church again. I'm not interested in its size or its location. Just give me a dozen people to pastor. I'll earn my own living, if necessary. Please, Father, let me be a shepherd again.

If there has ever been any doubt about my commitment, Father, I want You to know I'm Yours. I'll do whatever You want.

Kneeling there, Don took a stake and drove it into the ground, something he had not done before. Then he prayed again, "Father, I'm driving this stake as a sign that here, at this place, I've committed my life anew, and it's Yours for as long as You want to use it."[6]

He would later be offered quite unexpectedly a challenging position in a large church in Oregon.

And finally, I reached my own realization that my life had changed forever and, in a multitude of ways, for the good. I would write in my journal:

JOURNAL ENTRY— January 15

My first church service as a youth pastor today. I am truly in the ministry. This is a day I have dreamed about for five long years.

I awakened early at 6:00 A.M., prayed, and read from John. The service went well. Two people today commented on my reading of Scripture ("It was very alive and vital") and my public praying (a lady told me her son said I "pray like a Nazarene," which she told me was a compliment). I was much encouraged. I met a lot of the high school kids for whom I will be responsible. I'm very excited. I feel a singing internal confidence that Jesus and I will get the job done.

I haven't been depressed for a couple of months now, not

even sure exactly when it stopped. Has God really answered?

In so many ways I have changed, and been changed. It has been a marvelous journey, though also an incredibly painful one. But once again, for the first time in more than two years, I have tasted of his living water and his hidden manna. What is next? I don't know. I only know I look forward to the rest of my life whatever it will bring, whatever he will do—in me and with me.

Those, for me, were hard-won words and convictions. But they are well worth the winning.

In my thoughts, I keep returning to a text in John: "In the world you have tribulation, but take courage; I have overcome the world" (NASB).

Jesus was absolutely correct. In this world we do have tribulation, trial, anxiety, depression, loneliness, famine, disease, nakedness, peril, and sword. But none of it can separate us from him who has overcome this world. We can never lose his love, his forgiveness, his grace, or his loyalty.

Take heart in that truth. Jesus meant those words as potent comfort to all of us who struggle. So refuse to give in. As Paul told the Corinthians, "Be steadfast, immovable, always abounding in God's work. Your toil is never in vain." Encourage. Give and keep on giving. Share your life, your words, your heart. Do not give up the hope of eternal life and life with him. Someday we will be with him, and this world and its troubles will be a mere memory.

And in the midst of it all, realize that no matter how great the dark, we serve him who is Light. Together, we are achieving an overwhelming victory, one that Christ himself will applaud and say to us, face-to-face, "Well done, thou good and faithful servant." I will be there. And I pray, so will you.

Endnotes

1. C. S. Lewis, *The Horse and His Boy* (New York: Collier Books, 1970), 158–159.

2. Ibid.

3. Viktor E. Frankl, *Man's Search for Meaning* (New York: Pocket Books, 1963), 147–48.

4. Philip Yancey, *Where Is God When It Hurts?* (Grand Rapids, Mich.: Zondervan, 1977), 93–94.

5. William Styron, *Darkness Visible* (New York: Random House, 1990), 84.

6. Don Baker and Emery Nester, *Depression* (Portland, Oreg.: Multnomah Press, 1983), 95.

Additional resources on suffering and healing from Tyndale

LIVING WITH CANCER
Mary Beth Moster   0-8423-3679-6

MY JOURNEY INTO ALZHEIMER'S DISEASE
Robert Davis   0-8423-4645-7

WHEN GOD DOESN'T MAKE SENSE
Dr. James Dobson   0-8423-8227-5